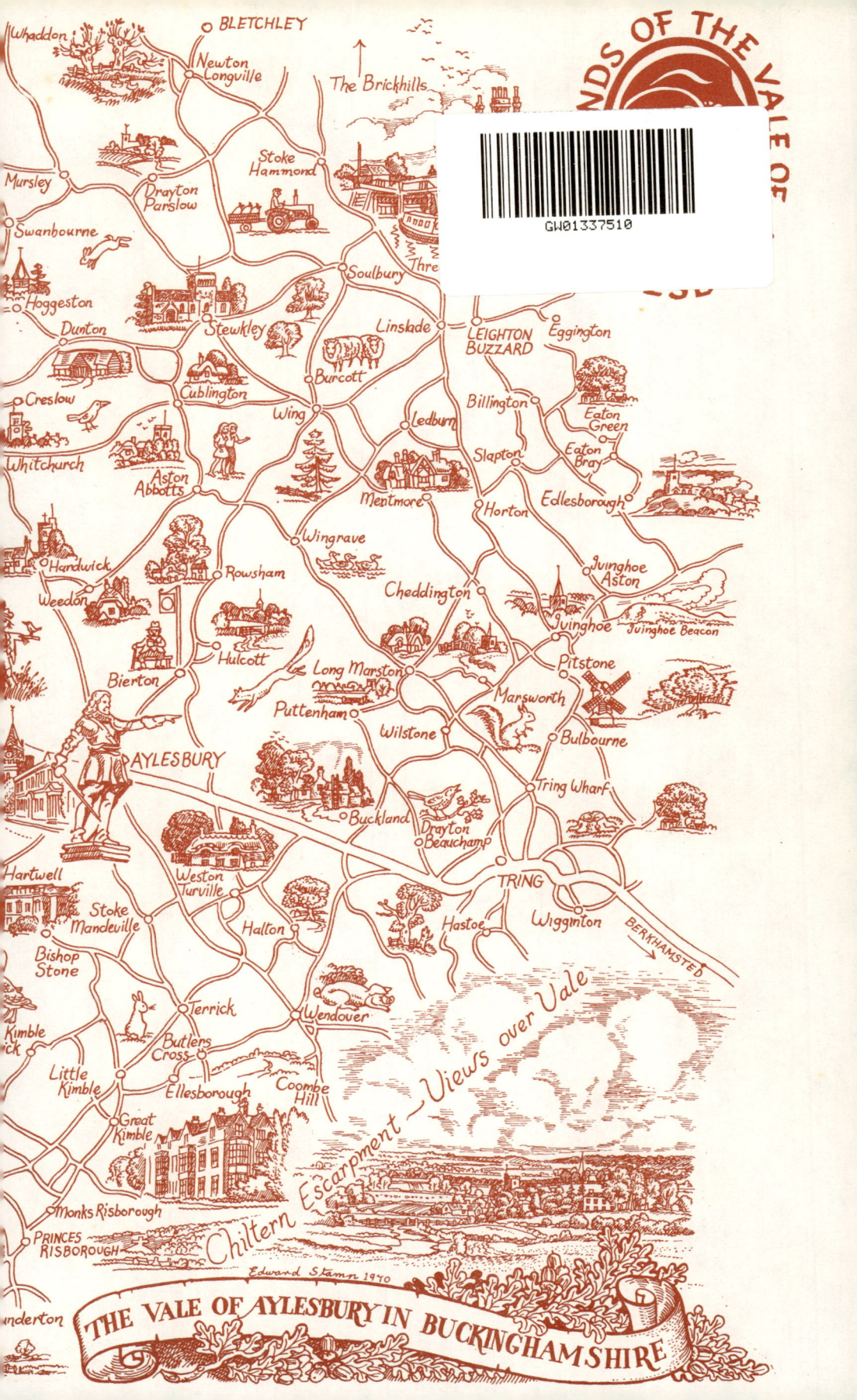

THE VALE OF AYLESBURY IN BUCKINGHAMSHIRE

Country like This
A BOOK OF THE VALE OF AYLESBURY

WILLIAM COBBETT *(see quotation on title page)*
The self-taught son of a labourer in Farnham, Surrey, he was born in 1762. He served as a soldier, but withdrew to Philadelphia to avoid persecution. Prosecuted for libel in 1797, he returned to London in 1800, where he edited a Radical paper. He was imprisoned and went to America again, 1817–19. He was M.P. for Oldham in 1832, and died in 1835.

Country like This

A BOOK OF THE VALE OF AYLESBURY
WITH A PREFACE BY Sir Arthur Bryant, C.H., C.B.E.

A friend had that morning taken him to view the beautiful Vale of Aylesbury, which he had never before seen; and the first thought that struck him on seeing the rich pasture was this: Good God! Is a country like this to be ruined by the folly of those who govern it?
WILLIAM COBBETT, *Rural Rides*, 1829

1972: THE FRIENDS OF THE VALE OF AYLESBURY

© 1972, The Friends of the Vale of Aylesbury
Designed by Peter Newbolt, Cley, Norfolk
Printed and bound in England by
Hazell Watson & Viney Limited
Aylesbury, Buckinghamshire
Distributed by F. Weatherhead & Son Limited
58 Kingsbury, Aylesbury, Buckinghamshire

Case-bound edition ISBN 0 9502501 1 2
Paper-back edition ISBN 0 9502501 0 4

Contents

Preface by Sir Arthur Bryant, C.H., C.B.E.   *page* 7

Foreword   9

Publisher's Note   11

Country like This   13

Select Bibliography   152

Acknowledgements   155

Index   157

SIR ARTHUR BRYANT, C.H., C.B.E.,
President of the Friends of the Vale of Aylesbury

Sir Arthur Bryant has for many years ranked as one of England's leading historians and authors. As well as having produced a number of outstanding books, including Makers of the Realm, Nelson *and* The Lion and the Unicorn, *he has for over thirty years contributed a weekly page on public affairs to the* Illustrated London News, *and features regularly in other major publications.*

More recently Sir Arthur has been actively concerned in the preservation of the Vale of Aylesbury for which he has long felt a deep affection. His interest in the history and character of the area is reflected in the work he has undertaken on its behalf, and it was at his suggestion that the Friends began collecting the material which has resulted in this book.

Preface
BY SIR ARTHUR BRYANT, C.H., C.B.E.

No comparable area in southern England – certainly none within fifty miles of London – contains a greater extent of unspoilt scenic beauty and rural peace. From Thame in Oxfordshire to Woburn in Bedfordshire lies a galaxy of lovely villages unsurpassed anywhere between the industrial Midlands and the Channel coast – the three Brickhills, Stoke Hammond, Soulbury, Aston Abbots, Cublington and tiny secluded Dunton, Stewkley, Hardwick, Weedon, Hoggesdon, Whitchurch, Oving, Pitchcott, Quainton, Dinton, Cuddington, the two Winchendons, Grendon Underwood, Chearsley, Long Crendon, Ashendon and the hill town of Brill. Of Quainton, by no means the most outstanding of the Vale's villages, with its exquisite Winwood almshouses, windmill, grey church tower, mellowed red-brick houses beneath its sheltering hill, I wrote during the War: 'In this place, with its still unbroken peace of centuries, the past is very near to the present. All English history – its strength, its sleeping fires, its patient consistency – are contained in its speaking silence.' An organic part of the permanent heritage of England, as near to perfection as anything of its kind at present existing, which has taken centuries to evolve and has bred successive generations of good Englishmen and today supports a highly efficient and up-to-date industry producing the most essential of man's needs – food.

If one stands on the summit of Muswell Hill – one of the noblest viewpoints in southern England – and looks eastwards up the Vale of Aylesbury it is hard to define the beauty of the Vale, for it is compounded of ever-changing light, but whether seen from the Chiltern escarpment or from the hills which rise like islands in the midst of its undulating plain, that checkered landscape of soft greens and browns, reflected clouds and far blue horizons is unsurpassed anywhere in England. It is the landscape which Rex Whistler painted and the deep-rooted countryside which A. G. MacDonell in his *England, Their England* described with such affection and understanding: 'the loveliest of English names, the Vale of Aylesbury. Pasture and hedge, mile after mile after mile, grey-green and brown and russet and silver where little rivers tangle themselves among reeds and trodden watering-pools.' With the county's southern part now given over to suburbia, industrial Slough and the western approaches of Heathrow, and much of the north to be swallowed up in the projected new town of Milton-Keynes-cum-Bletchley-cum-Wolverton, the survival of the Buckinghamshire landscape for future generations depends on the preservation of the Vale of Aylesbury. It should not be forgotten that of the ever-growing number of American and foreign travellers who come to England to see its historic sights, landscape and antiquities, a large proportion visit and pass through Buckinghamshire, and that rich agricultural vale below the Chiltern escarpment, with its buttercup meadows, hedgerow elms and red-brick and half-cast seventeenth-century cottages and soft blue horizons is often the first and unforgettable impression they receive of the English countryside.

The Vale is as rich in history as in beauty. It lies at the heart of the famous political shire which was the home of Hampden and Burke, of Disraeli and Rosebery, of the Grenville cousinhood which governed England through its most brilliant member, Chatham, at the apex of Britain's eighteenth-century glory, and, more recently, at Chequers, with its close associations with Cromwell, the country retreat of Britain's two great War Ministers, Lloyd George and Churchill. 'All this part of England,' wrote Disraeli, who loved it and delivered many of his speeches to gatherings of his farming constituents in Aylesbury, 'is history.'

Among the historic houses – in addition to countless humbler homes no less comely and ancient – are Chequers and Hampden, Hartwell and the wonderful fourteenth-century Doddershall – one of the oldest of England's habited houses; Oving, Ascott and Mentmore, Dinton, Tythrop, Dorton, Chilton and Wotton, and the great National Trust properties of Claydon and Waddesdon, with all their treasures.

Foreword

It is very difficult to define the character of a place; one can describe its physical appearance, its worth in terms of natural resources and important buildings, its industry and noted inhabitants – but the qualities that give it individuality cannot be explained simply in terms of history and geography.

The Vale of Aylesbury is one such area – peaceful, unobtrusive, but with a discernible atmosphere of its own – and when at the suggestion of their President, Sir Arthur Bryant, *The Friends of the Vale of Aylesbury* undertook to publish a book about their countryside, it was that unique character underlying the facts of its existence which they wished to express. In compiling the material, therefore, we looked to those people of many generations, occupations and interests who have known and loved this land, and who in some cases have left their own mark upon it. In effect, it is they who have 'written' this book.

Country like This does not claim to be a comprehensive survey of the Vale, nor yet a 'portrait in depth' of all its amenities; it does, however, through the medium of its people, attempt to give some insight into that quality of life which the Vale represents – and the preservation of which is of such critical importance today.

Sulgrave, 1972 MARY ELLEN HAIG

Publisher's Note

It would be impossible in the space permitted to name all those who have so generously contributed towards the publication of this anthology. A great amount of material, time and effort was freely offered, and to all who have assisted us in whatever capacity we express our warmest appreciation. We would also add that the material which we were unable to include will be kept by the Friends in their library, available to anyone who may be interested.

In particular, we wish to extend our gratitude to the following: our President, Sir Arthur Bryant, whose love for the Vale provided the inspiration for the book; Philip Jaques for his interest and advice; Shell-Mex and B.P. Ltd, for graciously allowing us to use the Rex Whistler painting of the Vale, both during the airport controversy and as the book cover; F. H. Shepherd for supplying copies of the Whistler painting and suggesting its use in opposing the recommendation of the Roskill Commission; Laurence Viney for printing the book and for his kind advice and support; F. H. Weatherhead for undertaking the distribution; Mary Hailey, Senior Assistant of the County Reference Library, not only for her work in compiling the bibliography, but also for two years of patient resourcefulness in supplying the answers to our many queries; Michael Farrar-Bell for designing the fritillary and tree symbols adopted by the Friends; Jean Bemis and Audrey Miles for researching copyrights and obtaining permissions; Jean Gowlett, Deborah Richardson, Caroline Wilmot and Diana Dewar-Drury for typing.

We wish to thank the Journal Committee of the Friends for their continuous support, both moral and financial, particularly Edith Wilmot, Chairman, and Susan Brockman, Secretary. Ruth Jordan for her expert editorial advice on the original Guide Book and supplement for *Bucks Life and Thames Valley Countryside*, and for assistance in compiling material on the villages; also Phyllis Spencer-Bernard and Diana Alderson. June Freeman for assisting with research and collation, Elaine Brunner for liaison work, and Peter Newbolt for designing the book.

We also wish to thank the following contributors: Ralph B. Verney, for allowing us to use the excerpt from his speech at Aylesbury during the Third London Airport controversy; E. Clive Rouse for preparing the article on the churches of the Vale; Richard Fitter and Susan Cowdy for their article on plants and wildlife; Max Davies for his article on the needlemakers of Long Crendon; Fred J. Taylor for his article on fishing; Desmond Fennell, for permission to quote from his telephone conversation with one of the *Friends*; Ruth Reynolds for her poems, 'Enigma' and 'Collared Doves'; and Miss

Esme James for the recipes of furniture and leather cleaners used at Chequers.

Lastly, and most important of all, we would express our indebtedness to our editor, Mary Ellen Haig, without whose dedicated work this book could never have taken shape.

The Old Rectory
Aston Sandford
1972

BETTIE MACPHERSON
Co-ordinator of Material
Vice-Chairman of the
Friends of the Vale of Aylesbury

Country like This

Two days later he was at Marylebone Station, quietest and most dignified of stations, where the porters go on tiptoe, where the barrows are rubber-tyred and the trains sidle mysteriously in and out with only the faintest of toots upon their whistles so as not to disturb the signalmen, and there he bought a ticket to Aylesbury from a man who whispered that the cost was nine-and-six, and that a train would probably start from Number 5 platform as soon as the engine-driver had come back from the pictures, and the guard had been to see his old mother in Baker Street.

Sure enough, a train marked Aylesbury was standing at Number 5 platform. According to the timetable it was due to start in ten minutes, but the platform was deserted and there were no passengers in the carriages. The station was silent. The newspaper boy was asleep. A horse, waiting all harnessed beside a loaded van, lay down and yawned. The dust filtered slowly down through the winter sunbeams, gradually obliterating a label upon a wooden crate which said 'Urgent. Perishable'.

Donald took a seat in a third-class smoker and waited. An engine-driver came stealthily up the platform. A stoker, walking like a cat, followed him. After a few minutes a guard appeared at the door of the carriage and seemed rather surprised at seeing Donald.

'Do you wish to travel, sir?' he asked gently, and when Donald had said that he was desirous of going as far as Aylesbury, the guard touched his hat and said in a most respectful manner, 'If you wish it, sir.' He reminded Donald of the immortal butler, Jeeves. Donald fancied, but he was not quite sure, that he heard the guard whisper to the engine-driver, 'I think we might make a start now, Gerald,' and he rather thinks the engine-driver replied in the same undertone, 'Just as you wish, Horace.'

Anyway, a moment or two later the train slipped out of the station and gathered speed in the direction of Aylesbury.

The railway which begins, or ends, according to the way in which you look at it, from or at Marylebone, used to be called the Great Central Railway, but it is now merged with lots of other railways into one large concern called the London, Midland and South Coast or some such name. The reason for the merger was that dividends might be raised, or lowered, or something. Anyway, the line used to be called the Great Central and it is like no other of the northbound lines. For it runs though lovely, magical rural England. It goes to places that you have never heard of before, but when you have heard of them you want to live in them – Great Missenden and Wendover and High

Wycombe and Princes Risborough and Quainton Road, and Akeman Street and Blackthorn. It goes to places that do not need a railway, that never use a railway, that probably do not yet know that they have got a railway. It goes to way-side halts where the only passengers are milk-churns. It visits lonely platforms, where the only tickets are bought by geese and ducks. It stops in the middle of buttercup meadows to pick up eggs and flowers. It glides past the great pile of willow branches that are maturing to make England's cricket-bats. It is a dreamer among railways, a poet, kindly and absurd and lovely.

You can sit at your carriage window in a Great Central train and gallop your horse from Amersham to Aylesbury without a check for a factory or a detour for a field of corn or a break for a slum. Pasture and hedge, mile after mile, grey-green and brown and russet, and silver where the little rivers tangle themselves among reeds and trodden watering-pools.

There are no mountains or ravines or noisy tunnels or dizzy viaducts. The Great Central is like that old stream of Asia Minor. It meanders and meanders until at last it reaches, loveliest of English names, the Vale of Aylesbury.

A. G. MACDONELL
England, Their England, 1957

The Manor of Aylesbury is a Royal manor, belonging to William the Conqueror, who invested his favourites with some of the lands, under the singular tenure of providing straw for his bed and chamber, and three eels for his use, in winter; and in summer, straw, rushes and two green geese; thrice yearly, if he should visit Aylesbury so often.

J. NORRIS BREWER
The Beauties of England and Wales, 1818

It seems to me that archaeology ought to pay more attention to headless horseman legends, particularly when they are related to stories about the building of a church. The *Iliad* gave a clue to the siting of Troy, the *Odyssey* has been found by Ernle Bradford to be a very accurate ship's log of a Mediterranean voyage, and it struck me that our folklore could provide similar pointers. When I made this suggestion I was still associating the legends with the pagan English or the Celts, and I supposed that heavily haunted churches would yield traces of their shrines. But there was the possibility that they overlaid much older hallowed ground.

In the 1920's, Watkins in his book *The Old Straight Track,* observed that many of our churches are situated on sight-lines between beacon points. He pointed out that primitive man, unlike his wagon-driving descendants, travelled straight whenever he could and always with beacon marks of one kind or another in sight. Earlier, nomadic peoples marked tracks with distinctive stones, and Dr E. A. Rudge, a geologist, identified about twenty years ago a chain of conglomerate stones, popularly known as pudding stones, which marks a track from the Wash to the Thames at Henley. The track connects flint mines and flint workings and passes through Chesham in Buckinghamshire where the church foundations rest on pudding stones and where there is a healthy tradition of a headless horseman. Rudge attributes the track to the Mesolithic period. This primitive method of marking a track may be compared with the use of similar stones by nomads in the Near East, Lapland and Australia, but it should not be confused with the more sophisticated use of sight-lines that Watkins first drew attention to.

Watkins invites his reader to test his observation by getting out an Ordnance Survey map and running a ruler over it from one beacon hill to another. I happen to live on a beacon hill in Buckinghamshire which is locally so distinctive that the Celts who gave it its first recorded name simply called it Bre – 'hill'. Remains from prehistory are scanty, but along with stories of headless horsemen there is a persistent legend that King Lud once lived in the village. Scholars who dismiss everything except literary evidence scoff at such tales, but there are some field and place-names which suggest that Lud, the water god whom the Romans called Nodens, has some associations with the hill. When I followed Watkins's invitation to mark sight-lines on a map from the hill towards the various marked beacon hills in the Chilterns, an astonishing number of churches were found to be located along these lines. The Lower Icknield Way, which passes at the foot of the Chilterns, connects a string of villages whose churches represent repeater stations for sight-lines crossing the Vale of Aylesbury from the hills above. These sight-lines frequently intersect, and the lattice of direct sight communication in the plain west of the Chilterns is extraordinarily complicated. Sceptics may dismiss the alignment of so many churches as merely fortuitous, but I am assured that the incidence of alignments exceeds statistical probability.

. . . My own guess is that this lattice of communication dates from the Megalithic Period, from the age of the first mathematicians . . . subsequent work by Professor Alexander Thom at Oxford, and Professor Lyle Borst of New York State University, Buffalo, confirm me in associating the lattice with Megalithic man. In 1967, Professor Thom, who is significantly a civil engineer and not an archaeologist, explored the geometry involved in the creation of stone and wood henges. These henges, popularly described as circles, are often egg-shaped or horseshoe-shaped in plan. Thom showed their shape was no accident and that they were achieved by the employment of a geometry which anticipated Pythagoras. He also found that the so-called circles employed a unit of measurement which was standard throughout Britain, and he defined this Megalithic yard as 2·72 feet. It's a nice coincidence that six of these Megalithic yards make an English rod, pole or perch.

. . . Last February Professor Borst published a preliminary paper in the American magazine *Science*. His offers of mathematical proof for Megalithic occupation of Christian sites seemed to support the hazy hunch I had derived from my folklore research. I wrote to him supplying him with horseman legends connected with the building of churches and was pleased to discover that he was already interested in the long barrow at Rodmarton. In June we met at Wing in Buckinghamshire, where I learned more of his ideas than he has so far committed to paper. Wing Church, like Brixworth in Northamptonshire, has a rare apse. It is a slightly irregular polygon and would once have had an ambulatory around it. Archaeological excavation dates the original church to the seventh century. The walls of the apse were rebuilt in the tenth century on the original foundations and some decoration and a new window were added in the fourteenth century. For several centuries the crypt in the apse was used as a charnel house, and local legend has it that it once contained the bones of a saint whose identity is significantly unknown.

The church and village of Wing are situated on a slight hill giving good horizons to the south and west and a panoramic view of the Chilterns to the east. Early versions of the name of the place are Weowungum and Wihthinge. Ekwall's *Dictionary of Place-Names* suggests that the name means 'Wiohtun's People', but my primitive Anglo-Saxon offers Weowungum as 'the dwelling-place of the idols', and Wihthinge as 'the henge of knowledge'. Putting my Anglo-Saxon aside, I must merely record that Wing Church is aligned with other churches in the Vale of Aylesbury and with Ivinghoe Beacon in the Chilterns. And setting aside for the moment the findings of archaeology on the site, I record simply as a fact that the shape of the polygonal apse at Wing conforms to a triangle of three by four by five Megalithic yards and that I witnessed Professor Borst make the measurements.

This particular three-by-four-by-five triangle produces the egg-shaped oval which Thom classifies as Type One. The oval shape is created by describing arcs from the point of the triangle, which is projected astride the axis line, the line of stellar observation. It commemorated, as it were, the observation point and provided a sanctuary around it, which was then marked by tree stumps or stones. Borst considers that the points of the polygon at Wing mark the sites of the original pillars. The wood henge at Arminghall in Norfolk, which was composed of eight wooden pillars, employs the same geometry but at twice the scale. Borst believes that the two structures are near contemporaries, and as the wood at Arminghall has been dated to 2500 B.C., he presumes a similar date for Wing. He believes that Wing is possibly the oldest continuously used religious site in Britain. While we were there he also checked the compass alignment of the nave and apse. He's fairly sure that the star employed at Wing was Bellatrix, and he expects his computation of its deviation to confirm the date of 2500 B.C.

Sceptics will find much of all this rather far-fetched. But there is more. Let us suppose for a moment that today's churches occupy pagan sites and that these were first occupied in the Megalithic period. Not every church, of course, reveals the complex geometry noted in some of our cathedrals, but it

All Saints' Church, Wing.

is significant that so many of them are situated on sight-lines. It's reasonable to assume that men who were capable of sanctifying their stellar observation points with a fairly complex geometry also practised ground survey work. Intermediate points on direct sight-lines of communication would need repeater stations. Watkins suggested that where distinctive topographical features were lacking trees of a distinctive nature were planted or observation towers were built. Initially such points would be maintained and guarded by the surveyor priesthood and in the course of time they would remain hallowed even though the reason for them had been forgotten. Successive invasions of different peoples would occupy these sites and devote them to their particular rituals.

It's possible that the legends of headless horsemen are a distorted and disguised relic of the men with their standard measurement of 2·72 feet, who first tried to survey this land. I confess that at this stage I can only offer this as a hypothesis. Much more research is necessary and the lattice of sight-lines requires statistical analysis to prove beyond doubt that the incidence of churches on sight-lines is more than accidental. Professor Borst, after a cursory study of the lattice for the Vale of Aylesbury, considered it likely that some of the sitings had stellar orientation, and the wild thought now occurs to me that the range of the Chilterns was once employed as a gigantic stellar computer.

Of course it can be argued that many of these ancient monuments have slightly altered their shape in the course of some years. It can be objected that even if some of our churches and cathedrals conform to Megalithic patterns, their geometry may have been borrowed. It can also be argued that those who built the churches didn't follow the precise outlines of the pagan shrines. Borst replies that builders habitually prefer to use existing foundations, that shrine-builders are inherently superstitious and that architects have a professional respect for previous structures.

. . . Close study . . . may yet prove that our recognised Megalithic monuments are only a part of the whole, that many others lie beneath our churches. If any archaeologist wants to start digging I'd be happy to send him a list of churches whose building was bedevilled and which are still frequented by a ghost who is not a ghost at all – merely a headless mathematician.

IAN RODGER
'Megalithic Mathematics',
The Listener, November 1969

A daughter, Osyth, was born at Quarrendon to Frithwald, King of Mercia, who had become a Christian. . . . Her parents married her to a Prince of the East Saxons, but with his consent she built a nunnery on some land which he gave her at Chich in Essex, and devoted herself to a religious life. A band of Danish pirates tried to make her renounce her faith; on her refusal she was beheaded at a fountain to which she was wont to resort for bathing. Then she rose, took up her head, walked with it in her hands to the church at Chich, and knocked at the door. Her friends took her body and buried it at Aylesbury, near which her home had been; but she appeared in a vision to a smith of that town, and asked that her bones might be moved to Chich, which was done after they had rested forty-six years at Aylesbury. St Osyth was canonised, and her day was kept at Aylesbury on October 7. A holy well, dedicated to her, was shown at Quarrendon. A pretty, homely custom kept up her memory. When the housewife went to bed (much alive to the danger of fire in the old thatched cottages) she raked out her hearth, made a cross in the ashes, and prayed to God and St Osyth to keep the house till morning safe from fire and water.

MARGARET M. VERNEY
Bucks Biographies, 1912

This pious King [Edward the Confessor] bore a more especial relation to these parts, by his frequent residence at Brill in Con. Buck, where he had a royal palace, to which he retir'd for the pleasures of hunting in his forest of

Bernwood. It is to this Prince, and to his diversion at this seat, that we must ascribe the traditional story of the family of Nigel, and the Mannor of Borstall on the edge of the said Forest. Most part of this tradition is confirm'd by good authority, and runs to this effect. The Forest of Bernwood was much infested by a wild boar, which was at last slain by one Nigel a Huntsman, who presented the Boar's head to the King, and for a reward the King gave to him one hyde of arable land call'd Derehyde, and a wood call'd Hulewood, with the custody of the forest of Bernwood, to hold to him and his heirs from the King, *per unum cornu quod est charta praedictae Forestae*, and by the service of paying ten shillings yearly for the said land, and fourty shillings yearly for all profits of the Forest, excepting the indictments of herbage and hunting which were reserv'd to the King. Upon this ground the said Nigel built a lodge or mansion house called Borestall, in memory of the slain boar. For proof of this in the Chartulary of Borstall (which is a transcript of all evidences in the reign of Henry VI, relating to the estate of Rede, Esq., then owner of Borstall, a large Folio in Vellam) there is a rude delineation of the sight of Borstall House and Mannor, and under it is the sculpture of a Man, presenting on his knees to the King the head of a Boar on the top of a sword, and the King returning to him a coat of arms, bearing Argent, a fesse gules, two crescents, a horn verd; which distinction of arms, tho it could not agree with the time of Nigel, yet it is most likely he did receive from the King, a horn, as a token and charter of his office of Forester, and his successors by the name of Fitz-Nigel did bear these arms. The same figure of a Boar's head presented to the King was carv'd on the head of an old bed-sted, lately remaining in that strong and ancient house: and the said arms of Fitz-Nigel are now seen in the windows, and in other parts: and what is of greatest authority, the original horn, tipt at each end with Silver gilt, fitted with wreaths of leather to hang about the neck, with an old brass ring that bears the rude impress of a horn, a plate of brass with the sculpture of a horn, and several less plates of brass with Flower-de-luces, which were the arms of Lisures, who intruded into this estate and office soon after the reign of William the Conqueror, has been all long preserv'd under the name of Nigel's Horn by the Lords of Borstall, and is now in the custody of Sir John Aubrey, Baronet, who has been pleas'd with great courtesie to communicate the notice of these things.

ROBERT GIBBS
Bucks Miscellany, 1891

Not far from Oxford there is a village which has no small place in the religious history of England. Some people would have us believe that our great reformer was never in Buckinghamshire at all. He had the living of Ludgershall for four years, and was at that time holding office in Oxford University.

Let us try to see how Ludgershall looked when (John Wycliffe) the most famous of its parish priests walked among his people, albeit he had not much time to give them. It was a scattered collection of wattle-and-daub farm-houses, huts and barns, still around the common green.

South-west of the church, which was not so very different from its present aspect, there was an old moated dwelling called King Lud's Palace, in the belief that the more or less mythical chieftain had given his name to the place; while on the north-east was Bury Court, which paid tithes to the great Priory of Bermondsey.

A little way off was Tetchwick, which had had a separate existence earlier than Doomsday, when it was possessed by Alwin, a rich theign whose descendants are still living. Ludgershall itself was owned by the Confessor's Queen Edith, who let it to a lady, Eddeva, but after the Conquest the rich Bishop of Coutances had it – this great Churchman had been with William at Hastings and had been politically rewarded with no less than 90 manors in Devon alone!

Beyond Tetchwick was Kingswood, still forest in Wycliffe's day. It has a tradition of a bower of Fair Rosamund. Her family, the Cliffords, had some land hereabouts, and in an old map of Bernwood there is a lane marked as 'Rosamund's Way':

> Bowers had Rosamund,
> About in England,
> Which the King for her sake made ...

says old Robert of Gloucester, and Henry II was so often at Brill that he granted two hides at Ludgershall for the service of keeping his hawks. Then there were the old land names – Illoem Piece, Dove House Field, Room of the Rush Piece – veritable fragments of the past.

Then came Ludgershall's foreign colony, in a field still called 'Friar's Mead', where the brethren of God's House at Santingfield, near Wissant, hard by Calais, had a small hospital, for young Henry II had granted these good brothers three hides of land (about 360 acres) and ten acres of woodland in Ludgershall.

As for the Manor itself, in Wycliffe's day it belonged to rather celebrated people.

About 1346, the year Crécy was fought, Sir John Molyns was confirmed in his possession of Ludgershall. He was a man who could not keep out of trouble, however, and when he, as King's treasurer, could not produce some money set aside for the French War, he was clapped into the Tower.

Being pardoned, he was made Queen Philippa's steward, with no better results, and this time he was outlawed. But his faithful wife, the Lady Egidia (in English, Gille) shared his imprisonment in Nottingham Castle. Their son, William, had their lands, after his parents had been provided for, and when the old reprobate had to be moved to Cambridge Castle, the son had to convey his father thither, under pain of forfeiting the lands if the

Some of the carvings, believed to be thirteenth-century, which form pillar-capitals in Ludgershall Church.

prisoner did not arrive!

Sir John died three years later, however, and his widowed Gille had her dower restored and was free to enjoy it in peace. We can imagine her visiting her son William at Ludgershall and listening to the startling eloquence of this new parish priest of theirs, with his tall, thin figure and flowing beard.

She sat on a stool or bench at the upper end of the nave (for the days of the regular pews was not yet), while her son and grandchildren stood beside her on the rush-or-hay-strewn pavement, and the village folk, according to rank, sat or stood on the floor. The Lady Gille wore the widow's linen wimple about her head and chin. Her son was a clean-shaven gentleman with hair cut to the nape of his neck, and a circular cloak, perhaps embroidered with the three red lozenges of the Molyns shield.

His wife, also seated, wearing the fashionable frontal of pearls and a full-skirted gown of, maybe, green and violet, had the children at her knee, like small copies of their parents.

The maids behind her would have flowing hair under silk wimples, for they would be daughters of other gentlemen, put out for education.

As for the village folk, the women wore decent gowns of hard-wearing stuff, generally much patched, and coarse linen aprons and hoods; while as for their husbands, we have only to go into Ludgershall Church today and examine those wonderful pillars to see what ordinary fourteenth-century men looked like, for there they are, in comfortable hoods coming down over their shoulders, linked arm-in-arm about the capitals as if playing a round game!

So there they all are, keeping the August festival of their church which made such a welcome break in labour – the day of Our Lady in Harvest – the feast of the Home-going of the Mother of God.

This great new teacher of theirs knew better than to instil into their childlike minds any disrespect for this lovely conception of the supreme woman which was the greatest civilising power that the world then knew.

'It seems to me to be impossible that we should obtain the reward without the help of Mary,' he tells them, and although his words might mean that he himself had not yet progressed beyond this point, yet they contained a tremendous truth.

Slowly but surely the Christian world was drawing away from the degraded idea of womanhood which the early fathers had so carefully inculcated and which was largely responsible for the brutal savagery of society during the Dark Ages. Mary, as the supreme pattern of the altogether lovely, was indeed the redemptress.

Sometimes, no doubt, Wycliffe's friends rode out to Ludgershall, especially that stout friend Peter Patershull, during the Long Vacation, when every ordinary man was supposed to give a hand with the harvest, if he had the chance. Wycliffe had been presented to Ludgershall on 13th November 1368, by Prior John Pawley, of the Hospital of St John of Jerusalem, while John de Wythernwick, former parson of Ludgershall, took on Wycliffe's old charge of Fillingham in Lincolnshire.

Thereby, of course, Wycliffe was so much nearer Oxford, where he had been Master of Balliol and Warden of Archbishop Islip's new Canterbury College. The Archbishop had been born at Islip, but he founded this college as a nursery for Christ Church at Canterbury, for that great institution had been decimated by the Black Death.

But Wycliffe had been removed from this new college because he was a secular scholar instead of a monk, and now he was a sort of Tutor at Queen's. It is even said that Geoffrey Chaucer, the poet, was one of his pupils. But he was much more than this. As King's Chaplain he had declared that the Pope had no right to tax England because of the base promise of the vile John to pay tribute, and his (Wycliffe's) account of the discussion is the first report of a Parliamentary debate in England. Luckily, the country sided with him, and another big step was taken in the history of England.

Then there was a fight with the Pope over the latter's claim to present to English livings, and Wycliffe went to a conference at Bruges to support the national claim, but by this time he had left Ludgershall, although his influence remained.

Later, when the tenets of Communism had unhappily brought national hatred upon the Lollards, brave souls still kept the torch alight in Buckinghamshire, and the most ancient Nonconformist church in Oxfordshire today seems to trace back to Wycliffe's Poor Preachers.

But it is the brave, kindly man himself we see when we go back to Ludgershall and look at the little window of his study over the church porch, and the ancient chest where he kept his vestments under the tower.

It was of Ludgershall that Wycliffe thought, we are sure, when he wrote, 'Whosover liveth best, prayeth best,' and that the best prayer of all is 'the simple paternoster of a ploughman that hath charity.'

ESTRITH MANSFIELD
'John Wycliffe's Life in a Village near Oxford',
Oxford Mail, 22 September 1933

Walter Giffard de Bolebec was the son of Osborn de Bolebec, and came over with the Conqueror. He was a great man amongst the Normans; the Conqueror gave him Whitchurch Manor, which was held under him by Hugh de Bolebec, his relative. Walter was one of the assessors of the Doomsday Survey, and for his zeal and attachment he held many manors under the Conqueror, no less than 107 in England, of which 48 were in Bucks. He was created Earl of Longueville in Normandy, and as is found in a charter of Henry I, was made first Earl of Buckingham about 1070, the ceremony at that period being purely military, consisting in being girt with a sword, and endowed with a payment from the County whence the title was given. He was faithful to the Conqueror and loyal to William Rufus, for whom he fortified his castles in Normandy. He was Chief Commander in the forces raised against Robert Curthose and his adherents. He died in 1103, holding Whitchurch; he was buried in the Abbey at Longueville, near Dieppe, which he had founded.

Walter Giffard, called Earl Walter the Younger, second Earl of Bucks, son of Walter Giffard de Bolebec, remained firm to Henry I, and fought nobly at Brennevillie, in 1119, against Louis, King of France, and Crispin, the famous Norman knight, when the French were defeated. He founded Notley Abbey – this Abbey was erected in the demesnes of Crendon Manor, for monks of a reformed branch of Augustine order, who came out from Arras, in France. They were, says Marsh, in Bucks Records, 'most rigid, wearing no linen, eating no meat, strictly silent, except at their devotions which filled up nearly their whole time, and they wore a white tunic.' It is said that (Walter) was assessed at 94 Knight's feet for the marriage of the King's daughter. Dying without issue in 1164, his lands were either escheated to the Crown or distributed amongst his relatives.   JOSEPH HOLLOWAY
Two Lectures on the History of Whitchurch, 1889

In 1290 Master John Shorne, who had been Rector of Monk's Risborough, was appointed to the living of North Marston which he held for some twenty-four years till his death in 1314. He was renowned far and near for his great piety and miraculous powers; 'his knees became horny from the frequency of his prayers.' He blessed the water of the 'Holy Well' still shown at North Marston, and endowed it (as was believed) with healing properties. In those days and long after, the Devil was a vivid personality, to be actually encountered and fought by the saints; as St Dunstan was said to have seized the Evil One with tongs, so Master Shorne caught the Devil and imprisoned him in his boot. For this reputed miracle he became an acknowledged saint. We are not told how the world was benefited while the Devil was kept in the boot; and whether North Marston in particular was freed from lying, malice and all uncharitableness; but the story became widely known and was carved in wood and stone, and painted in church windows. At North Marston in 1660, and perhaps later, 'there was a picture in glass of Sir John Shorne, with a boot under his arm like a bagpipe, into which he was squeezing a little figure of the Devil.' Two churches in Norfolk, Gately and Cawston, have representations of the Bucks saint; his fame spread from Kent to Northumberland, and in a poem of Heywood's, of the time of Henry VIII, a palmer, in telling of the holy places he had visited, classes Master John Shorne's shrine at Canterbury with St Denis's at Paris and St Mark's at Venice. But Shorne's chief shrine was at North Marston, where he died and was buried, and this became a famous place of pilgrimage; and such rich offerings did the pilgrims leave behind them that in the degenerate days of the monasteries the monks of Windsor bargained with the monks of Dunstable about the removal of the saint's bones. In 1478 the Dean of Windsor actually obtained the Pope's license to remove the shrine and the relics to St George's Chapel, Windsor; 'the monks published and bruited abroad what a sovereign qualified saint was come among them against all diseases spiritual and temporal'.

North Marston, however, continued to attract pilgrims, a stone image of the saint was there, and the Holy Well, famed for the cure of ague, then the most common form of illness in the county. An old rhyme says:

> To Master John Shorne
> That blessed man borne
> For the ague to him we apply . . .

Such numbers of invalids came to the waters that houses were specially built to receive them, and a finger-post on Oving Hill directed travellers to the famous well, which was said to have this inscription on the wall:

> Sir John Shorne, Gentleman born,
> Conjured the Devil into a Boot.

When the Lollards were being persecuted at Amersham some were condemned to perpetual prison, some thrust into monasteries, and others forced to make pilgrimage to the principal shrines in the county, St Rumbold's, Sir John Shorne's, and the Rood at Wendover. The Vicar of Wycombe got into trouble 'as he met certain coming from Sir John Shorne's, for saying they were fools and calling it foolatry.' A century later all England came to be of the Vicar's opinion. At the time of the suppression of the monasteries one of the Commissioners wrote to Thomas Cromwell that at Marston 'Mr John Shorne standeth blessing a boot, into which they do say that he conveyed the Devil.' This figure, which seems to have been of wood, was, with other of the more valuable relics, packed in a chest fast locked and nailed and sent up by barge to London. In the next reign Bishop Latimer, preaching of 'the Popish Pilgrimages', denounced the 'running hither and thither to Mr John Shorne, or to Our Lady of Walsingham', and 'the Boot' was amongst the relics most ridiculed by the Reformers.

In 1876 a successor of John Shorne, as Vicar of North Marston, Dr S. R. James, established a flourishing school there which he named Schorne College.

The history of the North Marston shrine is that of many others. Visits are paid at first to the place where a good man lived and died by those who knew and loved him; the custom spreads and a pilgrimage is authorised by the church, commended to the faithful, and imposed as a penance on heretics. Money (which has spoilt so many works of love) flows in and makes the shrine an object of greed and jealousy to rival monasteries, till the interests of the village are referred to the Pope at Rome; the avarice of the Court and nobles suppresses and confiscates whatever remains of the shrine; bishops denounce it, and Puritans deride, then the place and the saint fall into complete oblivion until the modern historical spirit revives curiosity, and the locality is once more interested in a kindly, tolerant way, in the story of its own bygone sanctity and greatness.

MARGARET M. VERNEY
Bucks Biographies, 1912

Dr John Colet, c.1467–1519, was Dean of St Paul's and founder of St Paul's School, Westminster. He left lands at Wendover and a number of neighbouring villages to be used for the upkeep of the school.

The Checquered Daffodill,[1] or Ginny-hen Floure, hath small narrow grassie leaves; among which there riseth up a stalke three hands high, having at the top one or two floures, and sometimes three, which consisteth of six small leaves checquered most strangely: wherein Nature, or rather the Creator of all things, hath kept a very wonderful order, surpassing (as in other things) the curiousest painting that Art can set downe. One square is of greenish yellow colour, the other purple, keeping the same order as well on the back-

[1] This flower, now known as the fritillary, has been adopted by the Friends of the Vale of Aylesbury as a symbol of the organisation.

side of the floure as the one the inside, although they are blackish in one square, and of a Violet colour in another; insomuch that every leafe seemeth to be the feather of a Ginny hen, whereof it tooke his name. The root is small, white, and of the bigness of halfe a garden beane.

The Ginny hen floure is called of Dodonaeus, Flos Meleagris: of Lobelius, Lilonarcissus variegata, for that it hath the floure of a Lilly, and the root of Narcissus: it hath beene called Fritillaria, of the table or boord upon which men play at Chesse, which square checkers the floure doth very much resemble; some thinking that it was named Fritillus: whereof there is no certainty; for Martial seemeth to call Fritillus, Abacus, or the Tables whereon men play at Dice. In English we may call it Turkey-hen or Ginny-hen Floure, and also Checquered Daffodill, and Fritillarie, according to Latine. Of the facultie of these pleasant floures there is nothing set downe in the antient or later Writer, but they are greatly esteemed for the beautifying of our gardens, and the bosoms of the beautifull.

GERARD's *Herbal*, 1597

The King's Head, which now belongs to the National Trust, was originally a monastery guest house, and this beautiful old inn dates from before 1450. The lounge has a magnificent Tudor window, with small leaded panes and some of the original stained glass. It is oak mullioned and made in four divisions, with transoms. It is a marvel that the glass has remained intact in a market town that has had such warlike associations. There are figures of golden angels with spread wings holding shields with the arms of Henry VI and Margaret of Anjou. It is thought they were put there at their marriage in 1445. The window has, too, the arms of Edward, Prince of Wales, who was killed at the Battle of Tewkesbury. Five emblazoned shields were removed from this window a century ago, three of which are in the British Museum and two in Westminster Abbey.

This splendidly gay window once overlooked the market square, but now it looks on a narrow alley hidden by the encroaching shops. The room has wall-posts of oak, black with age and smoke; and the beams spring from them. Above the entrance to the courtyard, with its timbered archway and stable and coach houses and steps leading to upper chambers, there is a modern oriel window. There is a seventeenth-century staircase with twisted balusters leading to the upper room here.

The storey above the oak-mullioned window overhangs, and is held by brackets. There are bright little window-boxes in summer, and always there is an air of well-being about the famous inn.

The King after whom the inn was named is Henry VIII, a constant visitor to the Guest House before his marriage to Anne Boleyn. Anne's father, the Earl of Wiltshire, was the Lord of the Manor of Aylesbury, and until her

Window of the King's Head Hotel, Aylesbury.

marriage Anne lived at the Manor House. When the monasteries were dissolved this Guest House was seized by Henry for the Crown, and the house given to the Earl of Wiltshire. Then it took Henry's name, and a painting of the King was on the hanging signboard until in recent years it was harmed by fire. In the seventeenth century the inn issued its own coinage, and some of these tokens can be seen in the Aylesbury Museum.

The inn walls are made of wattle and daub, and there is a portion stripped from its covering of plaster and exhibited under glass in the lounge to show its interesting construction. One can see the foundation of wattle with the daub spread over it to form a thick, strong wall. The meshes of the saplings are wide, and the skilful manner in which the walls were made is most striking.

Every inn has some kind of tale to tell, some legend of strange happenings, some memory of famous patrons, whether King or highwayman or soldier.

In the Civil Wars the inns of Bucks were used by King and by Parliament as the battles surged and places changed hands. They were the headquarters of generals, and Oliver Cromwell's name is associated with several large inns. He made the King's Head, Aylesbury, his headquarters when the Parliament troops were stationed in the market town. The old chair that was used by him is in one of the rooms. During recent renovations a hiding-place was discovered in the staircase, and there lay pieces of arms; a flintless horse pistol and cavalry musket as used in Cromwell's army.

ALISON UTTLEY
Buckinghamshire, 1950

John Holyman, Bishop of Bristol, 1495–1558, was born at Cuddington; presented to the living at Wing by Lord Dormer. Strongly against the Lutherans, he opposed the divorce of Henry VIII from Katharine of Aragon.

Whilst alluding to Aylesbury, I don't think it is generally known that the unfortunate Queen Anne Boleyn was often called 'The Fair Maid of Aylesbury'. Her father, Sir Thomas Boleyn, became Earl of Wiltshire; he inherited the Manor of Aylesbury through his mother, who was a daughter of Thomas Boteler. The Earl sold the manor to Lord Chief Justice Baldwin. The cause of his selling the manor was, he says in a letter to Thomas, Lord Bramwell: 'The truth is, that when I married my wife I had but fifty pounds a year for me and my wife as long as my father lived, and yet she brought me a child every year.' A writer of eminence says: 'This fair maid of Aylesbury is described as being of that singular beauty and tendernesse that her parents took all care possible of her education. Therefore, besides the ordinary parts of virtuous instructions, wherewith she was liberally brought up, they gave her teachers in playing on musical instruments, singing and dancing inasmuch that when she composed her hands to play and her voice to sing, it was joined with that sweetness of countenance that three harmonies concurred. Likewise, when she danced, her rare proportions varied themselves into all the graces that belong either to rest or motion.' These accomplishments, improved by the ease and self-possession she had acquired at the Court of France, captured, but could not secure, the affections of the salacious Henry, who, having conceived a passion for Jane Seymour, caused the Queen to be tried for adultery. This abominable charge rested on no other ground than some slight indiscretions, which her 'simplicity had equally betrayed to commit and to avow'. No proof of innocence could avail, however, with the king, she was condemned to die, and she expired on the scaffold. In one of

Norman font in the Church of St Mary, Aylesbury.

her affecting protestations, which she sent to her unfeeling persecutor, she thus expressed herself: 'From a private station you have raised me queen, and now you can raise me one step higher – to be a saint in heaven.' Anne Boleyn, when in the plenitude of her power, was a distinguished promoter of the Reformation, and all Englishmen should never be allowed to forget, that she was the mother of that truly great Sovereign, Queen Elizabeth.

J. F. K. FOWLER
Records of Old Times, 1898

The dictionary tells us that a cottage is 'a labourer's or villager's small dwelling'; we should certainly expect to find it inhabited by an employee rather than an employer, and we are quite entitled to exclaim: 'What charming cottages!' when we pass through many of our villages. But a point often forgotten is that the oldest, and probably the most picturesque cottages were not built for labourers at all. The old legal definition of a cottage gave us considerably less scope in considering what a cottage is, for we are told that 'by a statutue I, Eliz. cap 7 no man may build a house unless he lay four acres of land to it; so that a cottage is properly any little house that hath not four acres of land belonging to it.'

The amount of accommodation considered necessary for decent living has altered very largely in the last three centuries; learned men tell us that all forms of life develop from the simple to the more complex organism, and in like manner our dwellings have changed from one or two large rooms to a greater number of very small rooms. Whether this is altogether an advantage does not concern us now. The result has been that many moderately-sized houses have been sub-divided into two or more tenements, and the 'row' of two or three old cottages which we often see and admire was originally one long farmhouse, in which a large central chamber served as sole living-room for the farmer, his family, and labourers, and one or more smaller rooms at each end served as sleeping accommodation for all the household, and for storage of food. Often in such cases a single chimney-stack of old, thin bricks in the middle of the 'row' indicates clearly that it once belonged to a single tenement. That applied to the larger holdings of a parish; but before the days of Inclosure there were very many small holdings, of a dozen or more acre strips, scattered throughout the common fields. The effect of inclosure was to replace these small holdings by larger farms, upon which the small-holder became a labourer; but it is admitted that, although inclosure produced more food in the country as a whole, it diminished the number of people who were drawing a scanty subsistence from the soil. The single cottages which we now see, therefore, were often the homes of smallholders who were more or less compensated by the Inclosure Award for the land which they surrendered, and then became wage-earning labourers.

Even in pre-inclosure days there were labourers who possessed no more property than labourers possess today, but their homes were built of the rudest materials . . . clusters of mud-built huts, which had no second room. These have long since perished or have been re-built, so that, for the most part, the cottages which remain to us from the sixteenth and seventeenth centuries are the former houses of small-holders, copy-holders, and occasionally of comparatively rich free-holders, content to pass their simple lives in a dwelling which was comfortable indeed (according to the standard of that age) but allowed little opportunity for that privacy which is valued rather highly today. A good deal of smoke in the living room, stone floors, and abundant draughts were features common to all houses, great and small, in those days.

. . . The timber-framed house (or cottage as we know it) . . . has a very interesting history; in its earliest form it consisted of two pairs of curved timbers known as 'forks', or 'crucks', with their uppermost joints joined by a straight piece of timber which formed the ridge of the roof. In our county no building of this type exists today, although these words are being written in a house which contains one pair of such forks still in position, but there are several examples of the next stage in the development of this form of construction, where the tie-beam bracing the 'forks' was extended to the width of the 'forks' at their base.

. . . At a later period the curved principals, having no justification, were omitted. The interesting point about these designs is that the dimensions continued to be much the same throughout the sixteenth and seventeenth centuries; the 'forks', or the upright timbers, which succeeded them, were about $16\frac{1}{2}$ feet apart, although in Buckinghamshire this distance is often $15\frac{1}{2}$ feet. In any case it has a relation to the 'five and a half yards . . . one rod, pole or perch' of our school days. It was, in a word, the space needed to house two pairs of oxen.

. . . With this rough idea of the skeleton of the house, we may now consider its construction more closely. The foundations of rubble, large flints, etc., were brought about 18 inches above ground level; upon this rested horizontal timbers, or 'ground-plates', on which stood the upright principals of the bay. Their tops were joined by a tie-beam across the bay and by another horizontal timber which joined the ends of the bay and formed the wall-plate. The upright and horizontal timbers were often braced together with curved struts, and similarly in the roof the principal rafters were braced to wall-plate or purlin. As the upright principals could not exceed some 12 feet or so in height it was necessary that the upper floor should be partly in the roof, and the ceiling be formed at the level of the purlins. The upper floor was carried by a beam which joined the middle of the tie-beam at each end of the bay; this forms the ceiling-beam so general in the downstairs rooms of these houses, and with its stop-chamfer forms a useful aid to dating the structure.

. . . Having now sketched the skeleton of the house it remains to consider the walls. They had no structural value, they carried no weight, and were merely protection from the weather; they could therefore be made of wattle-and-daub, which was the cheapest form of walling before it became a forgotten art, or they could be filled with brick 'nogging'. Not infrequently a cottage is met with which exhibits both forms of wall, for the force of the weather below the line at which the wide eaves afforded protection tended to decay the wattle and daub, and the lower division of the house may be found filled with brick of varying sizes (indicating the various dates at which it was inserted), whilst the upper panels retain their original filling, which was certainly an efficient non-conductor of heat.

. . . Roofs in the Vale are generally of thatch, and where these have been replaced with tiles the pitch of the roof will generally indicate that it was originally constructed for straw, because thatch cannot be successful if the pitch of the roof is less than $67\frac{1}{2}$ degrees. Straw will only last if the rain runs rapidly off it without soaking in too much, and this can only be if the 'stulches', or layers of straw, are evenly and tightly packed, and the angle of the roof enables the water or snow to pass off rapidly.

Apart from the actual construction there is not much to guide one in dating these cottages; the fireplace has always been an open hearth 7 or 8 feet wide, and about 3 feet deep, with a seat on one side and a bread-oven on the other. It is rare indeed to find one nowadays on which the dog-irons are still used; wood is not so readily procurable, and the ease with which a hundredweight is burned in an evening is remarkable. In the Vale and away from the beeches the commonest wood is elm, which is not the best to burn on an open hearth without coal.

. . . It is usual now to find the open-hearth holding an open kitchen stove, with a diminutive oven on one or both sides; this enables coal to be used, and with a 'blower' hanging from the mantel beam the risk of smoke is reduced, but, on the other hand, pots and kettles become very black; they are hung from an adjustable pot-hook, which, in turn, hangs from a chain fastened to a bar across the chimney a few feet above the mantel-beam.

. . . Cottage staircases are very seldom contemporary with the house, the explanation being that they are eighteenth or nineteenth century replacements of some primitive kind of step-ladder which was the original means of access to the upper storey. When one sees a solid oak staircase it is certain that the structure containing it was never built as 'a labourer's dwelling'.

Windows are very seldom contemporary also, even when they are coeval with the house they have often been moved there from elsewhere; the nicely-wrought iron catch and neatly made lattice were only to be found in the best type of house, although they may now be seen in a much humbler abode.

Seventeenth-century houses never had fitted cupboards, and when we speak of the ample number of cupboards in a 'good old' house we are not carrying our memories back further than two centuries.

It was sometimes the practice to build one bread-oven for several cottages (there is, or was, an example of this at Chilton) – one can hardly imagine a more fruitful source of quarrelling between neighbours.

An important factor in the preservation of old cottages is continuous ownership; thus if an estate continues for many generations in one family (they are few today), generally speaking there is a tendency to preserve old buildings; they are not suffered to fall into such hopeless disrepair as necessitates their destruction. . . . In very recent years a great many estates have been broken up by sale to the sitting tenants, and in the course of a few generations this will have a bad effect in changing the character of the property so acquired. G. ELAND

In Bucks, 1923

Silver beaker of the fourth century A.D., part of a hoard of Roman silver discovered at Great Horwood in 1872, and now in the Aylesbury Museum.

Lord Philip Wharton of Winchendon, 1613–1696, left a trust to provide Bibles for the children of a number of parishes in Buckinghamshire and other counties. This trust still survives, and has been extended. To qualify for the gift the children must learn a portion of scripture by heart.

> The guests heere to the Bride-house hie.
> The goodly Vale of Al'sbury
> Sets her sonne (Tame) forth, brave as May,
> Upon the joyfull Wedding day:
> Who, dekt up tow'rds his Bride is gone.
> So lovely Isis comming on,
> At Oxford all the Muses greet her.
> The Nymphs are in the Bridall Bowres,
> Some strowing sweets, some sorting flowres:
> Where lustie Charwell himself raises,
> And sings of Rivers, and their praises.
> Then Tames his way tow'rd Windsore tends.
> Thus, with the song, the Mariage ends.
>
> MICHAEL DRAYTON
> 'The Argument of the 15th Song'
> *Polyolbion*, 1612

In the windowsill of the easternmost side window of the north aisle of Ickford church is incised a rough marking out of the game of Nine Men's Morris, which can be played on any flat surface. Relics of this popular pastime are now rare although examples still exist at Finchingfield in Essex and on a tomb at Dunster, Somerset. At the height of its popularity it could be found marked out on village greens, cathedral benches and in church porches, and it existed as a board game like chess. In *A Midsummer Night's Dream* Titania complains to Oberon that 'The nine men's morris is filled up with mud', so in this case it must have been cut in the turf.

The game was played on a board with coloured pegs. It is sometimes called Merelles. The pegs were of different shapes and were moved about on the surface which was marked with three squares and had twenty-four stations.

Each player had nine pegs and his aim was to capture his opponent's pieces and get his own into straight rows of three, when they could not be taken. Its name had amusing local variants: Morrice in Cornwall, Meg Merrylegs in Lincolnshire, Nine Men's Marriage in Derbyshire and Ninepenny in Oxfordshire. At Ickford the players obviously had to play standing up for the windowsill is elbow-high. A cement repair in the middle rather spoils the clarity of the outline. ROBERT GIBBS
Bucks Miscellany, 1891

The Church of Great Hampden is indissolubly linked with the name of John Hampden. It contains an elaborate monument by Henry Cheere which bears a relief of the battle of Chalgrove Field and a geneological tree which shows the connection between the Hampdens and the Trevors through 'Ruth, daughter of John Hampden, slain at Chalgrove Field'. There is some controversy about this monument. Although many believe it to be to 'The Patriot', it was actually to his descendant of the same name who died unmarried in 1754, leaving his estate to his kinsman, Robert Trevor, first Viscount Hampden, who gratefully erected the monument. One authority says John Hampden's grave is in the church, another says the precise spot is not known, but there is no doubt that he is buried there.

... There is no contemporary monument to Hampden in the church. John Hampden is believed to have been born in London although there is a tradition that he was born at Hoggeston in Bucks, despite the fact that his birth is not registered there. Oliver Cromwell and Sir Edmund Waller were his cousins. He attended the Grammar School at Thame and went on to Magdalen College, Oxford. His marriage took place in 1619 in Pyrton Church, Oxfordshire. He was returned several times to Parliament as Member for Wendover and later for Buckinghamshire.

His fame began shortly after the death of his first wife when, on January 25th, 1635, in Great Kimble Church, he protested against the payment of ship money in respect of the twenty shillings tax on his estate in the parish of Stoke Mandeville. Prolonged litigation followed which raised the validity of ship money. Judgement was given for the Crown against Hampden, but even his opponents admitted that the decision proved of more advantage to him than to the King's service. From that day, Hampden was known as 'The Patriot'.

Because he had such an intimate knowledge of passes in the Chilterns, he was able to be of service to Parliamentary troops when the King took up his Court at nearby Oxford and Prince Rupert overran the neighbourhood. He was involved in many of the skirmishes that took place around Aylesbury, and when Prince Rupert appeared with some 6,000 men at Stoke, two miles from Aylesbury, Hampden had to retreat to Brill, but not before the Parliamentary

Head of John Hampden, from the statue in Market Square, Aylesbury.

soldiers had demolished the apple pies baked by the wife of the Vicar of Wendover for Prince Rupert's men!

Hampden received his death wound at Chalgrove Field, fighting Prince Rupert and his men in a field of standing corn. The Earl of Essex arrived too late to pursue Rupert's troops who had already retreated to Oxford.

There has been much confusion and controversy concerning the nature of Hampden's wound. Some said he was killed by two carbine balls which struck him on the shoulder, and others that his own pistol exploded and shattered his arm. He left the field in agonising pain and tried to turn off to the Pyrton home of his first wife, but Rupert's cavalry stood between him and his objective. He then tried to get to his home at Hampden from which he had been almost continuously away since his marriage to his second wife, Letitia Vachell, two years previously. At Thame he was taken from his horse in a state of collapse and was carried to the house of Ezekiel Browne, where he died shortly afterwards.

His funeral was attended by all the troops that could be spared from the surrounding quarters. With their heads uncovered, their arms reversed and drums and ensigns muffled, they escorted him to his grave in Great Hampden Church adjoining his house. As they marched to the church they sang the 90th Psalm and, on their return, the 43rd.

The church and Hampden's old house are separated only by the roadway. The house, a low, battlemented building, is now used as a girls' school. It was in the brick parlour of this house that Hampden received the commissioners sent to arrest him. Perhaps the greatest beauty of Great Hampden is the fine avenue of chestnuts which was once the great carriageway to the house, but where grass now grows between the lines of trees.

In a nearby field there is a large stone cross, erected by Sir William Erle in 1863, with the inscription:

'For these lands in Stoke Mandeville John Hampden was assessed in twenty shillings of ship money levied by command of the King without authority of law the 4th of August 1635. By resisting this claim of the King in legal strife he upheld the rights of the people under the law and became entitled to their grateful remembrance. His work on earth ended after the conflict on Chalgrove Field, the 18th June, 1643, and he rests in Great Hampden Church. W.E. 1863'

ANNE JAMES
'Great Hampden and The Patriot'
Bucks Life, March 1967

With the opening of the year 1642 came an attempt on the part of the king, perhaps the most ill-advised of any that he made, to strike a blow at the leaders of the popular party. Pym, Hampden, Holles, Hazelrigg and Strode, were the men marked out for attack.

Sir Ralph [Verney]'s notes of the attempted arrest of the five members begin on Monday, January 3:

The king sent Mr Francis, a serjeant at armes, to Mr speaker with a message, and hee was cald in to the house and deliverd it at the barr, but hee was not sufferd to bring in his mace.

The message was thus, 'Mr speaker, the king commanded mee, uppon my aleagance, to repaire to you where you are now sittinge, and to demaund five gentlemen, members of this house, Mr Hollis, Sir Arthur Hazelrigg, Mr Pim, Mr Hampden, and Mr William Strood, and when they are deliverd, hee comanded me in his name to arrest them for high treason.'

Uppon this hee was comanded to withdraw, and the house resolved to send four members to the king, to let him know they had received the message, and would take it into consideration, but being there was noe charge deliverd in against those five gentlemen, they have not deliverd them, but have taken care to have them in a readinesse to answere any legall charge. And then the house comanded Mr speaker to call upp these five gentlemen by name, and injoyned them to attend de die in diem, till the house took farther order. The serjeant of the house was sent to tell sergeant Francis, that wee had sent to the king about these five gentlemen.

Mr Pim and Mr Hollis had there papers and studdies sealed upp, by warrant under the king's hand, and the house sent a serjeant at armes to arrest those that did it, and breake of the seales, and it was done accordingly. Wee sent to them (the lords) to joine with us, because they had protested with us to defend the privileges of parliament.

We have four independent accounts given by eyewitnesses of the next day's scene. Of these the most detailed is that of Rushworth, a young clerk-assistant lately taken into the service of the House, who, in the midst of the intense excitement, went on steadily writing at the table, as Sir Ralph, in much less comfort, wrote on his knee. His account completes our knowledge of the details of that memorable day.

Tuesday, January 4, 1641. The five gentlemen which were to bee accused cam into the house, and there was information that they should bee taken away by force. Uppon this, the house sent to the lord maior, aldermen, and common councell to let them know how there priviledges were like to bee broken, and the citty put into dainger, and advised them to looke to there security.

Likewise some members were sent to the four inns of court, to let them know, how they hears they were tampred withall to assist the king against them, and therfore they desierd them not to come to Westminster.

Then the house adjorned till on of the clock.

As soone as the house mett againe, 'twas moved, considering there was an intention to take these five men away by force, to avoyd all tumult, let them bee commanded to absent themselves. Uppon this, the house gave them leave to absent themselves, but entred noe order for it, and then the five gentlemen went out of the house.

A little after, the kinge came, with all his guard, and all his pentioners, and two or three hundred soldiers and gentlemen. The king commanded the soldiers to stay in the hall, and sent us word hee was at the dore. The speaker was commanded to sit still, with the mace lying before him, and then the king came to the dore, and tooke the palsgrave (his nephew) in with him, and comand all that cam with him, uppon their lives not to come in. So the dores were kept oppen, and the erale of Roxborough stood within the dore, leaninge uppon it. (This is a touch we have from Sir Ralph alone.) Then the kinge cam uppwards, toward the chaire, with his hat off, and the speaker steped out to meet him. Then the kinge steped upp to his place, and stood uppon the stepp, but sate not down in the chaire. And, after hee had looked a greate while, hee told us, hee would not break our priviledges, but treason had noe priviledge; hee cam for those five gentlemen, for hee expected obedience yeasterday, and not an answere. Then hee calld Mr Pim, and Mr Hollis, by name, but noe answere was made. Then hee asked the speaker if they were heere, or where they were. Uppon that the speaker fell on his knees and desierd his excuse, for hee was a servant to the house, and had neither eyes, nor tongue, to see or say anything but what they comanded him. Then the king told him, hee thought his own eyes were as good as his, and then said, his birds were flowen, but hee did expect the house would send them to him, and if they did not, hee would seeke them himselfe, for there treason was foule, and such an on as they would all thanke him to discover. Then hee assured us they should have a faire triall, and soe went out, putting off his hat till hee came to the dore.

Upon this the house did instantly resolve to adjorne till toomorrow at on of the clock, and in the intrim they might consider what to doe.

The Commons at once adjourned, says Mr Gardiner, 'With the sense that they had but just escaped a massacre. The orderly D'Ewes testified his opinion of the danger by stepping to his lodgings and immediately making his will.' That this opinion was shared by the country is shown by Lady Sussex's letter to Sir Ralph, written as soon as the news reached Gorhambury.

Thes distractede times put us all in great disorder, but i hope wee shall not bee kaillede; yet i think you are in greater danger than wee are in the contry; i pray god bles you with safety; your parlyment flyes hye; truly itt is a happy thinge, i thinke, the haue so much corige to stand to mentane ther right; the good tone of london it semes will do so to; truly the are to bee commendede; surely the kainges party will bee to weke; that he must yelde to the parlyment; i pray god derect all your harts to do for the bes for the good of us all; if wee now be ouer cam wee are undon for euer; i hope thos gentillmen the kainge woulde haue from your hose shall bee safe; the stand so much for the generall good that it was a miserable thinge the shoulde suffer; thes lettir will com safe, or else i shoulde not haue adfentiure to have sade so much. It was a blesede thinge thos gentilmen was from the parlyment when the kinge cam, he had ill counsill surly to com in such a way. I pray god all may conclude will, and that you may be as happy as you are wishede by your true frinde . . .

FRANCES PARTHENOPE VERNEY
Memoirs of the Verney Family during the Civil War, Vol. II, 1892

King Charles the First to Parliament came,
Five good Parliament men to claim;
King Charles he had them each by name,
Denzyl Holles and Jonathan Pym,
And William Strode and after him,
Arthur Hazelrigg Esquire
And Hampden, Gent, of Buckinghamshire.

The man at the gate said 'Tickets, please,'
Said Charles, 'I've come for the five M.P.'s.'
The Porter said 'Which?' and Charles said 'These:
Denzyl Holles and Jonathan Pym,
And William Strode and after him,
Arthur Hazelrigg Esquire
And Hampden, Gent, of Buckinghamshire.'

In at the great front door he went,
The great front door of Parliament,
While, out at the back with one consent
Went Denzyl Holles and Jonathan Pym,
And William Strode and after him,
Arthur Hazelrigg, Esquire
And Hampden, Gent, of Buckinghamshire.

Into the street strode Charles the First,
His nose was high and his lips were pursed,
While, laugh till their rebel sides near burst, did
Denzyl Holles and Jonathan Pym,
And William Strode, and after him
Arthur Hazelrigg Esquire,
And Hampden, Gent, of Buckinghamshire.

HUGH CHESTERMAN
King Charles the First
'Speech Practice' ed. by G. Colson, 1959

We cannot but acquaint you, that you may make it knowne to the House of Commons, if you please, in what miserable condition this country is at this time, the King hath sent into these parts about 12 or 1400 of his Forces, commanded as wee are informed by the Earl of Cleaveland, who is accompanied with the Lord Shandose, the Lord Crawford, Sir John Byron, and others of Note, who according to the knowne Law of the Land, pillage and plunder all the towns where they come, they murder our neighbors that

Harvest, seen from Whiteleaf, in the days before combine harvesters.

make but any defence to preserve their goods, one woman (among the rest) bigge with child, who could make no great resistance; they cut in peeces what household goods they cannot carry away; they sweep cleane divers of our pastures, leaving no Cattell behind them, and that no cruelty might be left unexercised by them, they have this day fired a Country Village called Swanbourne, in 7 places of the Towne, for no other reason but because they were not willing to be plundered of all they had, and guarded the fire so carefully with al their forces divided into severall parts, that no neighbors durst adventure to come to quench it, all the while it burned our Forces in this Garrison consisting only of Foot, saving one troope of Horse, we were not able to encounter with the Enemy, nor relieve our neighbors thus despoyled, but yet to interrupt that, which to them is a sport, we drew out some Forces in their sight as far as with safety we could, whereby they have not acted this day all the mischief they intended to execute before night, but what they have undone today, wee expect they will, ere they leave us, make up, for they are now so strong that they quarter at Buckingham and where they please, in these parts without resistance. We wish the Parliaments Army were so accomodated, that this Country (which hath hitherto bin, and yet is most ready to serve and obey the Orders of the Houses) might not be destroyed and made utterly unable to contribute unto it, before we can be relieved by it, but relying upon God's providence, and the best means which may be afforded to preserve us. Wee rest, your very loving Friends to serve you, JOHN WITTEWRONG, THO. TYRRILL. Ailsbury, 16 May, 1643.

Letter directed to Col. Hampden, Col. Goodwyn, and
read in both Houses of Parliament, May 18, 1643,
quoted in ROBERT GIBBS
Bucks Miscellany, 1891

On the 14th of June, 1645, Charles I quitted the field of Naseby, Northamptonshire, leaving behind him 800 dead, 4,500 prisoners, all his artillery and ammunition, and a battered, mauled, but triumphant Parliamentary army.

That night, or maybe the night after, Cromwell stayed at Dinton House, the residence of Simon Mayne, and in his mood of stern joy gave his sword to the house in perpetuity. For Simon Mayne, a man who had thrown in his lot so wholeheartedly with Parliament, and who, in 1642, as one of a Grand Jury, had presented an address to the King, asking him to dismiss his army, Cromwell's visit and gift was a peak in his career. Three years later he sat in the painted chamber of Westminster Hall as one of the judges of his king, and during the ten days of the trial Simon Mayne missed only one sitting. A 'great committee man, where-in he licked his fingers' he signed the death warrant with alacrity.

Thereafter, on a cold January morning, Charles I was paraded from St James's Palace to Whitehall on foot and at two o'clock a man in a visor severed his head with one blow, whilst another man, equally anonymous, held up that severed head and exclaimed: 'This is the head of a traitor!'

At that moment, with the Puritans in complete and utter control of the kingdom, the return of the monarchy to England seemed an impossible dream. But return it did; and in the June of 1660 Simon Mayne surrendered himself to the Sergeant-at-Arms. Already he was an abject, broken man. Four months later, at the Old Bailey he was standing trial as a regicide and was condemned to death. But that was all the satisfaction his judges got for, unable to walk to the scaffold, Simon Mayne died in the Tower of London 'from gout, with fever and convulsion fits' on April 13, 1661. His body was delivered to his wife – his second – 'for interment in the country without ostentation' – at St Peter's, Dinton.

Meanwhile, across the fields, in the elegant, half-timbered Waldridge manor house, Sir Richard Ingoldsby, another regicide, and one who had served in the Parliamentary army, was enjoying a very pleasant life. He, too, had been appointed a king's judge, but though he had signed the death warrant he had never made an appearance at the trial. Later, after vigorously supporting the Protector's son, Richard, he had entered into negotiation with the agents of Charles II. Then, from secret to open collaboration, he had, at the head of a body of troops, apprehended the obdurate, anti-royalist, General Lambert, and marched him to London.

So, at the coronation of Charles II in the April of 1661, this man . . . who had claimed that Cromwell himself had set the pen between his fingers and moved his hand so that it had written his signature – 'he making all the resistance he could!' – was created a K.C.B.!

During the years to come, Sir Richard represented Aylesbury in four parliaments, and before he died in 1685, had a progeny of seven grandsons and seven grand-daughters.

Meanwhile, away from this cheerful household, there had been at the interment of Simon Mayne, his one-time secretary, a man called John Biggs. Although his employer was dead he had, at 32, no particular worries about his future. A secretary of repute, he could easily get new employment: even with Sir Richard Ingoldsby whom he had served at various times in the past. But after the funeral this well-educated man became subject to deep melancholic introspection, and to remorse. Eventually, he took his abode in an old hut, and there, subsisted on what the charitable people of Dinton gave him. At his belt he carried three bottles; one for strong beer, one for small beer, and a third for milk. But the only things he ever asked for were strips of leather to mend his apparel and boots which he had fashioned himself.

And in this manner he lived for thirty-six years; to the wonderment and speculation of the entire countryside. Then, in 1696, upstanding to the last, this old man with the serene countenance, a man 'without a trace of moroseness, severity or vulgarity in his person' died.

By then, his clothing, patched and mended with strips of leather, had reached an enormous, tatterdemalion thickness, whilst his shoes had swollen to ten times their original size: each one being composed of over 1,000 pieces of leather! One of these monstrous shoes is in the Ashmolean museum, whilst the other is, or used to be, at Dinton Hall.

John Biggs was buried in St Peter's churchyard, and with him went the secret rumoured by so many people. Was he one of the visored executioners of Charles I? No-one knew then, no-one knows now. All that is certain is that three Dinton men played parts in an event that shook all Europe, but that each followed an entirely different destiny.

ERIC RAYNER
'Three Men of Dinton',
Bucks Life, June 1967

We had two active Parliamentarians in Crendon. The first was a Henry Cannon, who later moved up into the hierarchy during the Interregnum. His father was a bailiff on the Windsor third of the manor, later renting the demesne farm. Henry joined the army at the beginning of the war, fighting under Cromwell in the celebrated 'Ironsides'. The second was John Randolph, who had a Dormer copyhold, and with five others became 'collectors of money' at Aylesbury. They had the task of collecting levies from the surrounding districts. Each village had to pay a monthly contribution and the principal inhabitants were also made to contribute to the cause. Haddenham's share was £8 17s 6d and we paid about the same amount.

In the Public Record Office are the accounts of Edward Lenton of Notley, who was a barrister of Gray's Inn. The methods of present tax collectors are nothing compared with the means employed during the Civil War. The unfortunate man had to pay £30 poll money and £10 for his son, which was paid to an officer of the Exchequer. He was obliged to contribute £50 for a forced loan for 'the distressed subjects in Ireland' which was guaranteed 'upon the faith of Parliament'. Unfortunately that faith only paid back £25. He was obliged to loan two horses which were sold in London for £40 and 'he has never since got the horses nor any sight of them'. Worse was to come; when the Earl of Essex was quartered at Thame, Edward Lenton paid £30 for 'his 5th and twentieth' but was summoned to Aylesbury 'by the committee there and compelled to pay three score and ten more'. At the same time: 'Captain Andrew with all his officer and troup of horse lay at the house ten days and ten nights free quarters, their horses eat up not only my pastures but much of my hay ground and some of my corn and feasted his friends at my house.'

He was also compelled to pay a fixed monthly contribution of £1 7s which was a seventh part of what was paid by the town. Also odd contributions for straw, hay, beans, mattresses, shovels, etc. He bitterly complained of having to make 'so great payments out of so small means'.

JOYCE DONALD
Long Crendon, A Short History, 1971

The small garrison of new raised Militia at Aylesbury had been moved to some quarter which was more closely threatened, and the town and the rich pastures which surround it were left unprotected. Thither Prince Rupert marched with a force of some thousands of horse and foot, and, after some days past in securing for the King's use much of the produce of the Vale and despoiling and laying waste much more than he secured, entered and possessed himself of the town. Here after one more day of free quarter in Aylesbury, during which the inhabitants were made to suffer all sorts of outrages from the soldiers, he received intelligence of the approach of a brigade of the Parliament's troops from Stony Stratford. Rupert, probably afraid of attempting a defence within the walls of a place, however well adapted by its situation for defence, where the townsmen were all his enemies, and having in his front a country over which his cavalry could act with great advantage, left there but a troop of horse and two companies of foot, and marched out with all the rest of his force to meet the advancing enemy. But he had not gone further than the brook, about half a mile to the northward of the town, where there was then no passage but a bad ford, swollen by the rains, when he found himself checked by Balfore's horse and foot in column, on the opposite bank. After the first volley or two, Rupert charged across the ford, and, breaking through Balfore's two first lines of infantry, plunged into the centre of his horse, who were flanked on the right by Charles Pym's troop. And here a sharp conflict began. Sir Lewis Dives came up with the Prince's reserve, and Captain Blanchard with Balfore's; the musketry of the foot, the carbines and petronels of the cavalry, swords and poleaxes all doing the work of death, and the soldiers of all arms mixed and fighting in one close and furious throng. It lasted thus but a few minutes. The King's troops were driven back across the stream, and Rupert rallied on the other side, only to lose more men from the fire, and to receive a charge in return, which drove him back in confusion towards the town. In vain did the troops hurry down to his support. The townsmen rushed forth upon his rear, with whatever arms haste and fury could supply to them, and Rupert began his retreat towards Thame, before the mingled troops and populace, who, however, after slaughtering the hindmost for above a mile, did not venture further to pursue among the enclosures, a force still superior to their own. In this action some hundreds of Rupert's men fell, and of the Parliamentarians above ninety.

ROBERT GIBBS
A History of Aylesbury, 1885

... We must remember the history of Buckinghamshire, of John Hampden, of Milton, of Wilkes, all fighters against tyranny in its various forms, all pledged to the inalienable right of the little man to live in his home unharassed by the tyranny of the Public Interest in whatever guise – ship money, despotic government, rigged elections or the tyranny of technology under which we are suffering today. We must remember the little men who have no memorial except the majestic arches of Stewkley Church, the elm trees which give colour and glory to the Vale landscape, the deeply-rooted communities of our Buckinghamshire villages with their tradition of neighbourliness and courtesy and mutual respect. And we must say to Parliament and the Government with the clarity of absolute conviction, that the arithmetic of Roskill simply will not do; that every organisation in Buckinghamshire, statutory, democratic and voluntary, representing every shade of opinion in the County, utterly rejects its inhumanity, and demands that the blight of this threat to our countryside and our homes should now be finally removed, and an airport if one is needed should be constructed at Foulness or any other suitable coastal site. Yeomen of Bucks, strike home!

RALPH B. VERNEY
*Extract from a speech made in Aylesbury, 1971,
when Chairman of the Buckinghamshire County Council*

Norman arches at St Michael and All Angels, Stewkley.

Benjamin Keach (1640 to 1704) was a well-known Baptist minister. He was born of poor parents at Stoke Hammond, and baptised in the parish church; later, under the influence of John Russell, a Baptist minister at Chesham, he was baptised again at fifteen and worked as a tailor. At the age of nineteen Keach became a zealous preacher; in 1664 he was seized and imprisoned for preaching at Winslow, where he had found his wife, Jane Grove, and where he ministered in a humble little chapel in Pillars' Ditch. He had not long been released when he was arrested again for writing and printing the *Child's Instructor*, a Baptist catechism. He was tried at Aylesbury before Sir Robert Hyde, sent to prison without bail, and sentenced 'to stand in the pillory at Aylesbury in the open market', and again in the pillory at Winslow, where his 'seditious and venomous book' was to be burnt before his face, and he was fined £20. Another time, while he was preaching at Winslow, the little meeting-house was surrounded, Keach was seized, and with much violence and indignity tied across a horse and so taken again to Aylesbury. The bitterness of the trial was increased by the knowledge that the Rector of Stoke Hammond, who had been appointed under the Commonwealth, and had just conformed, was the one to inform against him. In 1668 Keach took refuge in London, but he was a man of too much originality to please any authority. He published a collection of hymns and first introduced congregational singing in his chapel, which the London Baptist Association of 1669 condemned as 'a carnal formality'. His brother, Henry Keach, a miller at Soulbury, had sometimes a meeting in his mill of one hundred, 'all mean people', as their persecutors described them; and from thence John Griffith and Jonathan Jennings were sent to Aylesbury gaol. The name remains in Keach's Meeting House and burial ground at Winslow, one of the oldest dissenting chapels still existing in Bucks. His little persecuted flock met at Granborough, Oving and North Marston in private houses, taught by John Hartnell, a thatcher of North Marston.

MARGARET M. VERNEY
Bucks Biographies, 1912

We will wear the weeping willow, for a twelve month and a day.
And if anyone should ask the reason why I wear it
Tell them my true love is gone far away.

A 'numbering' song sung by an old man of Bucks

From hence, we proceeded on the road towards Oxford; but first turned to the right to visit Aylesbury. This is the principal market town in the county of Bucks; tho' Buckingham a much inferior place, is call'd the county town. Here also is held the election for Members of Parliament, or Knights of the Shire for the county, and county gaol, and the assizes. It is a large town, has a very noble market for corn, and is famous for a large tract of the richest land in England, extended for many miles around it, almost from Tame, on the edge of Oxfordshire, to Leighton in Bedfordshire, and is called from this very town, the Vale of Aylesbury. Here it was that conversing with some gentlemen, who understood country affairs, for all the gentlemen hereabouts are graziers, tho' all the graziers are not gentlemen; they shew'd me one remarkable pasture-field, no way parted off or separated, one piece of it from another; I say, 'tis one enclosed field of pasture ground, which was let for £1,400 per ann. to a grazier, and I knew the tenant very well, whose name was Houghton, and who confirm'd the truth of it.

It was my hap formerly, to be at Aylesbury, when there was a mighty confluence of noblemen and gentlemen, at a famous horse-race at Quainton Meadow, not far off, where was then the late Duke of Monmouth, and a great many persons of the first rank, and a prodigious concourse of people.

I had the occasion to be there again in the late Queen's reign; when the same horse race which is continu'd yearly, happen'd again, and then there was the late Duke of Marlborough, and a like concourse of persons of quality; but the reception of the two dukes was mightily differing, the last duke finding some reasons to withdraw from a publick meeting, where he saw he was not

A meet of the Old Berkeley Beagles at Shelswell Park.

like to be used as he thought he had deserved.

The late Lord Wharton, afterwards made duke, has a very good dwelling at Winchenden, and another much finer nearer Windsor, call'd Ubourn. But I do not hear that the present duke has made any additions, either to the house or gardens; they were indeed admirably fine before, and if they are but kept in the same condition, I shall think the duke's care cannot be reproach'd.

... We went on from Aylesbury to Thame or Tame, a large market town on the River Thame: This brings me to mention again the Vale of Aylesbury; which as I noted before, is eminent for the richest land, and perhaps the richest graziers in England: But it is more particularly famous for the head of the River Thame or Thames, which rises in this vale near a market town call'd Tring, and waters the whole vale either by itself or the several streams which run into it, and when it comes to the town of Tame, is a good large river.

DANIEL DEFOE
Letter VI
A Tour Through England and Wales, 1724–26

John Martyn, 1699–1768, botanist and physician, owned an estate at Lower Winchendon. He was co-founder of the London Society of Botanists, and published many important medical and botanical works. His son, Thomas Martyn, was Rector of Ludgershall, 1774–76.

Elder Fflower Wine

Take twice six gallons of ye Chrystall Rill,
That issues clearest from the craggy Hill.
Add thirty pounds weight of the glistering grains
The dulcet produce of barbadian canes.
O'er the clear fire then let it simpering play
Till its sixth part be flown in steam away.
Then scum it well & cooling let it stand
Till it will warm & yet not scald your hand.
Of Ale Yeast then fourspoonsfulls of it pour
And of the Syrup spoonsfulls of it four
That the brisk Lemon or fair Citern yields
The fragrant product of hesoerian feilds.
The work of fermentation then begun
Throw just two quarts of Elder flowers on
Cleared from their stalks & gathered in the sun.
Nice care to stir it every morning take
Till free from fermentation Rests the settled cake.
Then close confine it in the untainted Sun
Till her pale course the moon has three times run.
Then when its sun bright stream will clear the sight
Confine it stricter yet allow it light
Close in its glasey prision let it be
Till the hor Autum sets the captive free
Then as you quaff it gratefully you'll own
The french Champagne by British art outdone.

JANE TYRINGHAM BERESFORD
Recipe Book
Nether Winchendon, 1722–27

On either side of the main Aylesbury to Oxford road on the western boundary of Bucks lie the 'Witchert Villages'. Haddenham is the most extensive of these and contains the best examples of the use of the very localised building material known in this area as 'witchert' or 'witchett'. Other villages include Cuddington, Nether Winchendon, Chearsley, Long Crendon, Dinton, Ford and Bishopstone.

Wherever one turns in Haddenham there are walls, some up to ten feet high, topped with tiles – formerly, thatch was used instead of tiles but there are hardly any examples of this to be seen today. It is well worthwhile spending some time in Haddenham walking along the many picturesque cobbled footpaths between the witchert walls. Here, away from the roads and their associated noise and rush, you can breathe in the character of the old village.

Try walking from Church End through Fort End to Town's End along these pretty alley ways on a quiet summer evening and you will know that machines and concrete have not yet dominated the whole country.

Witchert – the word is probably a corruption of 'white earth' – is a stiff, white clay-like substance associated geologically with the Upper Portland Limestone which comes within a foot or so of the surface in, for example, Cuddington. In some gardens this 'white earth' may be found three to four feet below the surface, overlying a layer of hard limestone. When it is mixed with a little water it can be worked up into a plastic material which adheres firmly to boots, shoes, hands and spades, and seems to find its way into everything, including the house, drying out as a white crust which is very difficult to remove. According to those who can remember, the 'wallers', as the witchert builders were called, were always covered in mud; one local character was known as 'Muddy' Taylor.

There are, however, few alive today who have the skill to use witchert as a reliable building material. The long-lasting evidence of former workmanship and the qualities of the material itself are shown by the wealth of walls, cottages and even larger houses built almost entirely of witchert. I lived for some years in a cottage, the walls of which are made entirely of witchert taking the whole load of elm and oak beams as well as a tiled roof. This cottage, which is listed by the Royal Commission on Historic Monuments as being of probably early seventeenth-century origin, has outlived many a brick-built one and will last for another century, as long as the walls are not allowed to get wet.

Witchert buildings have a character all of their own, due undoubtedly to the plastic nature of the material. The characteristic rounded corners of the buildings and the flowing contours of the walls give a Spanish effect which is accentuated by the pantiles often fixed to the tops of the high walls to throw off the rain water which could destroy the wall in one season.

According to one who has actually used this material to make good the old walls in his village, the material is worked and used as follows. The topsoil is cleared and the witchert dug out and transported to the building site where it is spread out and mixed with chopped straw. Then there follows the hard and dirty job of turning the pasty material – water may have to be added to get the right consistency – over and over again, all the while treading it to work the straw in as evenly as possible. In the meantime a foundation is built in the normal way. This foundation may be of limestone or brick and may be about eighteen inches above ground level, the purpose being to keep the dried-out witchert off the damp ground, since it relies on its being dry for its strength.

At this point the muddy mixture of witchert and straw is flopped down on the foundation to a height of no more than two feet at a time, in much the same way as one might build up a layer of compost in a neat heap in the garden. The fork which was used to apply the muddy witchert was normally three-pronged and had flat tines. After leaving this layer to dry out a few days, the edges were chopped with a sharp spade, and a smooth surface thus obtained which was either left raw, giving a very pleasing texture, or rendered with a layer of lime mortar or roughcast. Each layer was built on the preceding one in much the same way as a house martin builds its nest.

It is amazing that walls of over twenty feet high were built in this way. Stability was achieved by building walls of up to two feet thick at the base, tapering to perhaps one foot thick at the second floor.

Witchert used as a building material must not be confused with 'wattle and daub' which depends on a wooden structure for its strength, the 'daub' being merely a filler material. Dry witchert walls of two feet thick are immensely strong, and a great deal of hard work is needed to knock them down or to cut holes for any new doorways or windows – ask any local builder who has worked on such walls. Moreover, it has the advantage of high thermal insulation, and no cottage is cosier than the witchert cottage of these parts with its open fireplace and old oak beams.

There are interesting examples of witchert cottages along the High Street in Haddenham. One old cottage has an oak-framed 'cruck' construction, the panels of which are almost sure to be filled in with witchert, and another close by it, called 'The Bone House', has witchert walls rendered with roughcast which in turn has been decorated with various symbols, including a spade and three-pronged fork.

Many of the old cottages are still thatched, like those in Ford, Cuddington, Long Crendon and the Westlington end of Dinton. In one of the back lanes of Cuddington, there is a fine example of an unrendered thatched building showing the pleasing continuous curves that may be achieved in witchert construction. Further along the same lane may be seen the remains of a decaying wall which was once thatched – in sharp contrast to the well-maintained corner building. Several interesting and beautiful witchert cottages surround the upper village green at Cuddington, and an old one-time inn at the lower green affords an example of a large dwelling-house built almost entirely of witchert.

Few of those who visit the lovely Priory at Nether Winchendon realise that the rustic brown cottages in that village are mainly timber-framed witchert. In past years most of the cottages in this village and some in Cuddington have been colour-washed with a tan limewash, indicating that they belonged to the Bernard estate.

Although, sadly, many of the old walls are being allowed to fall into disrepair through sheer neglect, it is rewarding to see the sympathetic preservation of both buildings and walls by those who realise that their properties are, in respect of the 'white earth' used to make them, unique to this corner of Buckinghamshire.

NORMAN GOOD
'The Witchert Villages of West Bucks'
Bucks Life, January 1967

Witchert walls, Haddenham.

John Westcar was a celebrated grazier, and the occupier of Creslow Pastures, near Whitchurch. He was a leading exhibitor at the Smithfield Club Cattle Show, at the end of the last and beginning of the present century. It is said that he was the first grazier in this district who introduced a system of conveying fat cattle to the London Market, otherwise than by road, for he made use of the canal and its boats for the purpose; thus we find in Mr Gibb's *Local Occurrences*, date December 10, 1799 – 'Mr Westcar of Creslow, sends a fat ox to London for the Christmas Show, it travelled by the Wendover canal, it was two days on the journey and reached there safe, thereby losing no flesh from the easy way it travelled. This was considered quite a novelty at this period.' Again we read, 'Dec. 25th, 1799 – the ox fed and shown in London by Mr Westcar, was remarkable for its weight and size; it gained the first prize and was sold for £100; it weighed upwards of 241 stone; its height was 6 feet 7 inches; length 9 feet; girt 10 feet 1 inch.' Between the year 1799 and 1821, Mr Westcar received 42 prizes for different animals shown at Smithfield. He was a just and good man, and lived to a good old age. He was found dead in the Great Ground at Creslow, supposed to have fallen from his horse, on the 24th of April, 1833. Two trees were planted to mark the spot. He was in his 84th year when he died, and he left £1,500 in charities, divided between the poor of Whitchurch, Cublington, and Souldern, Oxon.

JOSEPH HOLLOWAY
Two Lectures on the History of Whitchurch, 1889

Buckinghamshire, in common with many other counties, was once rich in windmills. During the inter-war years there were still about a score of mills to be found dotted about the Buckinghamshire landscape. Time has reduced this total to very small proportions. Year by year the remaining mills continue to decay, and when their condition deteriorates to the point of danger they either collapse or suffer that last indignity – demolition. Two mills, Brill and Pitstone, have benefited from the interest of restorers. Both these mills – post mills – represent examples of the earliest type of mill design. Two examples of later mill design seem to merit particular attention. They are the smock mill at Lacey Green – the oldest of its type in England (A.D. 1650); and the fine tower mill at Quainton.

Each of the three types of mill derives from the miller's need to make the mill sails face into the wind. The superstructure of the post mill was rotated around its central upright post. The smock mill was a wooden tower, usually eight-sided. Its sails were attached to the cap which could be revolved by the miller when the wind changed direction. The tower mill was a development of the smock mill, and its body was constructed of a more durable stone, brick or rubble.

An old farming manual provides some interesting facts concerning these powerhouses of the past. Although many mills had wooden gears the millwright's work called for considerable precision and skill. The angle of the plane in which the sails moved depended upon the mill's location. On exposed heights it could be as much as 15 degrees from the vertical, but on level ground it could be as little as 8 degrees.

Mill stones appear to have revolved five times for each turn of the sails. A wind of about $12\frac{1}{2}$ m.p.h. gave 12 turns of the sails per minute, and produced approximately 4 h.p. A minimum wind strength of $7\frac{1}{2}$ m.p.h. was required to drive a mill, and the safe maximum wind strength was 20 m.p.h. Beyond this limit there was a danger of the stones running hot and setting the mill on fire.

A mill's grinding capacity depended upon the area of the sails and the size of the millstones. The larger the stones the more power they required.

For example, a wind strength producing 3 h.p. would revolve millstones of a yard across some 200 times a minute. In an hour these would grind 120 lb. of bread flour. The weekly output of the Bledlow Ridge mill in 1798 was 15 sacks or some 4,200 lb. of flour.

Once a mill is demolished and the physical evidence disappears it soon becomes difficult to piece together its history. Since the last century many mills have disappeared and our knowledge of them has to be gleaned from old directories, parish histories and similar records. One useful source of information concerning mill sites is to be found in the pre-war series of Ordnance Survey $\frac{1}{4}$-in. maps. Vanished mills were situated at Aylesbury, Walton (2), Brill (2), North Crawley (2), Farnham Royal, Grove, Hartwell, Hulcott, Mursley, North Marston, Padbury, Prestwood, Princes Risborough,

The seventeenth-century windmill near Brill.

Quainton, Towersey, Turweston, Whitchurch and Wing. Insufficient evidence has survived to tell us what sort of mills they were.

The Wing mill was in such a condition in 1798 that it was due 'to be taken down immediately', but it appears to have survived at least until 1864 when Richard Harris was the miller. At this time the miller at Mursley was John Carr. He lived at the Windmill Inn and combined his milling with the trades of publican and maltster. Whitchurch mill stood at the junction of the Oving–North Marston road. Here in 1776 the unfortunate miller John Flowers (the old spelling of flour was 'flower') was struck by lightning. In 1808 another miller, John Johnson, was buried on the mill ground. After a severe fire on 7th December 1890, the mill does not appear to have worked again.

Windmilling never assumed the importance of watermilling in the county, and watermills always outnumbered windmills. In 1798 out of a total of 119 mills in the county, 97 were watermills. Generally speaking, the grinding capacity of a watermill was twice that of a windmill, and the watermiller had a more reliable element on which to depend. As far as the windmiller was concerned, the final blow came when steam engines were developed to the point where they could satisfactorily provide the driving power for mill stones. By the end of the last century many windmillers had also installed steam mills.

. . . A mill was mentioned at Stewkley in the early fourteenth century, but the only visible trace of a mill to be found today is the stump of the brick smock mill, built in 1839, which stands by the lane leading from the Carpenter's Arms. Three carved bricks above the door indicate that the mill was built by three brothers named Tofield. Twenty-five years later a John Tofield was the miller. He could easily have been one of the builders. There were two mills operating in Stewkley during the last century, but all trace of the second has disappeared, and its location is uncertain.

. . . Quainton mill stands at the top of the village green looking out over the Vale of Aylesbury. This is undoubtedly one of the most impressive mills in the county, and its history is equally fascinating. The hundred foot tower which rises for six storeys above the green was started in 1830 by James Anstiss. When the structure reached the third floor work ceased, and a temporary roof of thatch protected it while James went on a visit to America. Some years elapsed before he returned and the work was completed. To celebrate this event one of the workmen – a John Dubney – is said to have climbed the mill's highest sail to drink to its success. Dubney's risky climb was attended by more danger than he realised. The brake was not on and the sails could have turned. The fine tower was made from handmade bricks. No scaffolding was used externally as the tower was built chimney fashion from the inside. The Anstiss family has a long tradition as millers. Thomas Anstiss, Junior, worked one of the two Quainton mills which were used in 1798 before the tower mill was built. He was clearly aware of the miller's difficulties. A brief record quotes him thus: 'No corn can grind without some wind. Perhaps when wind no corn to grind.' After some hundred and thirty years the mill built by James is still in the Anstiss family. The mill which once stood at North Marston is also said to have been owned by a miller named Anstiss.

The remains of the Great Horwood mill give us a few clues as to its former glory. An old postcard shows that its lofty tower was finished with a neat ogee cap and fitted with a fantail. Each sweep or sail had two rows of adjustable shutters. The mill was refitted in the late nineteenth century. During the 1920's the tower became a private dwelling. For this reason its tarred tower survived, largely intact, until the last war. When Great Horwood airfield was constructed the mill, situated on its perimeter, became a potential danger to aircraft and the tower was dismantled – almost. The surviving portion provides, under quieter skies, a shelter for pigs. The Haddenham mill was also a wartime casualty. It too stood in the way of an airfield and was completely dismantled.

The credit for introducing the windmill to the English countryside is usually given to the returning Crusaders of the thirteenth century. We know very little about the technical details of the first mills, but from them man evolved a technology in wood which in a later age was translated into iron and steel. It is salutary to reflect that the complex gearing of the modern motor car owes its ancestry, in part, to those silent powerhouses of the past.

JOHN N. T. VINCE
'Powerhouses of the Past'
Bucks Life, March 1967

One very respectable gentleman farmer, in the Vale of Aylesbury, assures us (and this was confirmed by others) that their meadows were by nature so rich, that watering, as it is practised in other counties, made their crops of grass so rank and coarse, that two acres of their natural meadow-grass, not watered, though less in quantity, was superior in quality; and worth more than two acres and a half of similar quality of meadow, in a watered state.

WILLIAM JAMES AND JACOB MALCOLM
General View of Agriculture in Bucks, 1794

On Christmas Eve, 1753, about two thousand people of the village and neighbourhood met at midnight in the rector's garden at Quainton with torches and lanterns, to watch for the budding of the thorn, which is said to be a true and veritable descendant of the famous Glastonbury Thorn. Now, the peculiarity of this thorn is, that it buds on the 24th of December in each year, ready to be in full bloom on Christmas Day, and to die off at night. The object of the meeting was to decide between 'Old Style and New Style'.

Previous to 1753 a confusion of dates prevailed, consequent on different methods of computing time. In order to correct this error, an alteration to the extent of eleven days was necessary to be made. By the statute of the 24th of George II, it was enacted that the natural day next following the 2nd of

September should be reckoned the 14th of September, and the several days succeeding the 14th of September should be reckoned in numerical order, according to the order and succession of the days used in the present calendar.

Hence we have Old May Day as well as May Day; Old Michaelmas as well as New Michaelmas; and the like of other old and new days in the calendar. So great was the ignorance of the people, that they were under the impression that Government, by altering the calendar, had taken some advantage of them, and a cry arose, 'Give us back our eleven days.'

At Quainton, it is said that great superstition prevailed on the subject, and much discontent. It was determined to settle the question, not by the provisions of an Act of Parliament, but by an appeal to the laws of nature. Christmas Day, 1753 (new style), was to be the day to prove whether the Act of 24th George II, did really alter the time or not. It was therefore agreed that if the thorn in the rector's garden showed signs of budding on the 24th December (new style), at midnight, then, both by the laws of man and laws higher, the next day would be the true Christmas Day. But the thorn did not show any signs of budding. It was therefore resolved that the next day was not the true and proper Christmas Day. It was not kept, either by the attendance of the people at the services of the church, or in the usual festivities. It is further stated that so deep rooted was this aversion to the new Christmas Day, that on Old Christmas Day Divine service was performed in this and the neighbouring churches, in order to appease the people, who, on this, the usually-appointed day, kept Christmas festivities as in the 'good old times' of their fathers.

ROBERT GIBBS
Bucks Miscellany, 1891

Dr George Lipscomb was a native of Quainton. His father, Dr James Lipscomb, was in early life a medical officer in the Royal Navy. He married Mary George of Grendon Underwood; they resided at one time in Grendon, and at Quainton. James Lipscomb died in 1794, and was buried at Quainton Church where a memorial is erected to his memory. Dr George Lipscomb, their son, came and resided here (Whitchurch), he occupied the villa on the east side of the High Street, known now as 'The Sycamores' . . . here he followed his profession and was considered the Village Doctor. It was during his residence here that he began to write 'The History of Buckinghamshire', which has made his name so famous to us. In Dr Lipscomb's time postage was expensive, paper and wood engravings dear, nevertheless he persevered; his work is a grand one, but it exhausted all his means. Eventually he left Whitchurch to live in London, hoping thereby to be able to secure aid to help him in his difficulties, but he ultimately died in Westminster, in abject poverty, and but for the kindness of a Mr Gyll of Wraysbury, he would have

The Church of St Mary, and Winwood Almshouses, Quainton.

been laid in a pauper's grave. However all honour to Mr Gordon Gyll, he saw that he was decently buried and paid all expenses connected therewith. His place of burial is not known. His wife pre-deceased him and they left no issue. His history was published in 1847.

JOSEPH HOLLOWAY
Two Lectures on a History of Whitchurch, 1889

'A very populous village,' wrote Lipscomb in 1802 of Long Crendon, 'in which more than a thousand persons are said to be employed in the manufactuory of needles. The buildings are, however, extremely irregular and the streets remarkably dirty.' We have forgotten the needles now, and think more highly of our buildings – seventy-six, no less, are listed in this parish by the Ministry, and of these three are rated Grade I.

When Lipscomb wrote, Long Crendon had been a needle-making centre for about two and a half centuries and had only another half century to run. But neither he nor the needlemakers themselves knew that the writing was on the wall.

Curiously, this rise and fall has been poorly documented as far as the ordinarily interested citizen is concerned though no doubt scholarly sources exist for the tapping. Even the *Victoria County History* finds no more solid

57

reference than a pamphlet of reprinted articles from a Redditch newspaper of 1897, entitled *Notes on a Decayed Needleland*, by William Shrimpton.

This modest reference, however, is a rewarding document with a fine Victorian ring of resolution, embellishment and morals. An introductory chapter by a pseudonymous 'Arrowside' leaves us in no doubt about the place of needlemaking in the economy:

'Out of this quiet spot in days of yore came the tapestry and cross stitch, the tambour and the netting needles which high born dames in many a stately chamber and hall wrought with dainty device into the marvellous and fairy like creations of the period. Surgeons' needles for all the wounds of the world sped forth on their errand of mercy from this quiet spot, and not a navy rode proudly on the waters without paying tribute to the skill of the Long Crendon sailmakers' needles.'

William Shrimpton himself sets the tone of his narrative in his very first, nostalgic page. Recalling (in 1897) that as a boy he used to 'linger at either the shop doors or the windows, listening to the dull thud of the stamp or the hum of the wheel', he goes on:

'But where are the workers now who once made the village famous? . . . What has become of the merry mirth-making which used to hold its own at festive times? What has become of the holiday seekers, the majority of whom were bent on draining to the very dregs the cup of pleasure?'

This theme of past merrymaking recurs over and over again in the little book's pages. 'The laughter of the merry monks' used to ring in the ancient hall of Notley Abbey. The schoolgirls met by 'Arrowside' were 'singing merrily on their way home to dinner'. The needleworkers of 1736 are described by one Henry Young (a then inhabitant) as making themselves 'at times very merry at the ale house', and tending to be popped into the stocks in consequence. 'Arrowside' finds the needlemakers a pretty merry bunch at all times and shakes his head sadly over the fact that being 'a musical and laughter loving race, they preferred playing the clarionet, and joking with the farmers, and working quietly when in the mood' to making their fortunes. Their general frivolity, in fact, emerges, in William's view, as the root cause of their decline.

Getting down to business after amiable digressions in the direction of place names, a Roman cemetery on the Aylesbury Road and the mottoes of the church's peal of eight William tells us at length that:

'Of the origins of the needle trade at Long Crendon little is known, but it is nevertheless true that one Christopher Greening understood the mysteries of the art. From old records we find that he came to Long Crendon in the reign of Queen Elizabeth, 1560, and that needles were then made in the village. Some of the inhabitants, no doubt, were taught the art of needlemaking by Christopher Greening.

Some attribute to him the honour of introducing the trade into the village, but needlemaking was known to others in the village at that time as well as to Christopher Greening.'

Very quickly, it seems, the Shrimpton family came to the fore in the trade and remained there until it decayed – indeed until afterwards, as they still flourish in Redditch. One of the most formidable of a notably lusty tribe must have been 'old Thomas' in 1800 whose 'sixteen sturdy children, eight sons and eight daughters' were 'nearly all employed at needlemaking'. Ten Shrimptons were engaged as principals in needlemaking in 1814, and William lists thirty-five, including sons (but not daughters), in 1840.

We are told little about the trade in the seventeenth and eighteenth centuries, except that it was largely a cottage industry. William does tell us something about the transport side, however, apparently about mid-eighteenth century.

'... when a quantity of needles had been made, sufficient to pay the travelling expenses to and from London, and to allow as well a fair profit for time and outlay, a journey was undertaken by one of the more wealthy of the makers. The cost of the journey was about seven guineas and the time taken to accomplish it (50 miles each way) from seven to ten days. The journeys were made by the stage coach from Oxford, the only available route of reaching the metropolis. When the needle maker made the return journey it was customary for him to bring home a stock of wire. Some of the accounts at that time were balanced as follows: part payment in wire and part in coin of the realm.'

It was about this time that Henry Young was noting the dissipated manners of the needlemakers in the alehouses. But they were evidently developing more refined tastes, too.

'We find that in 1790,' writes William, 'the Harrises and Shrimptons were not only prominent as makers of needles, but were prominent as bellringers, which is not at all surprising when we consider the musical tastes they possess [*sic*].'

By the end of the century transport arrangements had altered, but not much:

'When Business necessitated a journey to London, the nearest point to meet a coach for the great city was the village of Tetsworth, six miles distant. At that time about 20 coaches left Oxford daily for London ... the Harrises and the Shrimptons were in the habit of travelling once to London in about ten weeks.'

The rot was imminent now, though not yet apparent.

'In 1810 ... the various processes of manufacture were very primitive. The processes connected with the making of sail, packing, sewing and surgeons' needles were carried through with hand labour. No stamps were used, such as are in use now . . . Sail needles were forged on the anvil, and on account of the way in which they were made were very costly. With regard to the pointing, hardening and scouring, these processes were very tedious and helped to increase the cost of labour. Very little provision was made by the makers for increasing the trade of the village, nearly all of them being given to following the various sports and pastimes which were then held, including bull baiting, cock fighting, pugilistic encounters, and attending wakes and fêtes.'

It must have been about this time that some unnamed entrepreneur, 'a gentleman of unlimited wealth,' says 'Arrowside', offered to finance the equipment of Notley Mill on the River Thame for needlemaking by water power. Why was this sensible move not made? 'The causes,' says William,

'were in the first place due to there being little or no competition, and secondly to the desire on the part of the manufacturers for pleasure.'

They do seem to have been a little worried, though, and after one or two abortive starts one Jonas Shrimpton visited Alcester, Studley and Redditch to see what was going on. This was, in 1824, no mean journey. He went by stage coach through Oxford to Banbury, thence to Stratford-on-Avon and thereafter on foot.

Jonas found that at Alcester needles were being made by machine stamp, and he came back warning the manufacturers of Long Crendon to have a care. 'The advice was not heeded,' says William, 'consequently the old course of pleasure was still indulged in.'

He does have a good word to say for one manufacturer, however, about this time, who seems to have been a regular Samuel Smiles character:

'It was about 1830 that young John Harris commenced business on his own account. The course he pursued in the management of his business was different from some of the others. He endeavoured to the best of his ability to produce needles of the best quality . . . Harris's needles were known to be reliable owing to the fact that John put reputation and character before self. Envious makers might be jealous of his success, but what cared John for their carpings and criticisms?'

The example did not spread, alas! and the exemplar himself is not excepted from the general censorship thirty years later when the industry virtually left Long Crendon altogether.

Perhaps Jonas Shrimpton's warnings were being heeded in a way he did not expect. William reports the removal of no less than seven young Shrimptons from Long Crendon to Redditch around 1830. Even these, moving as you would think with the meritorious intention of bettering themselves, do not escape the censor:

'Golden opportunities for improving their positions had been put in their paths . . . London merchants and traders were frequently at Crendon with offers of money to the needlemakers so that their workshops could be fitted up with suitable machinery . . . Alas! how many of us, like these needle makers have rejected offers made to us of improving our position.'

In 1844 there was a removal on an almost far western scale when one John Shrimpton with wife, children and work people, numbering eighteen in all, left for Redditch.

'Farmer John Kirby provided the two horses and covered wagon that conveyed the adults and children, and Farmer William Carter provided the four horses and covered wagon that conveyed the whole of John's household furniture, stock-in-trade and trade appliances.'

The journey took three days.

Methods at Long Crendon continued primitive and steam was not used there until 1848, several years, perhaps a decade after it had been adopted in Redditch. The Midlands were surpassing Long Crendon in welfare, too. Measures were adopted there to combat 'grinder's asthma' which carried off most needle pointers by the age of 40. Not so in Long Crendon, where not surprisingly recruiting a labour force was becoming difficult.

In 1850, however, things took a surprising turn for the better. A new firm, Kirby, Beard & Company, previously purchasers of needles, set up a brand new factory with an 8-h.p. steam engine and modern machinery. One Andrew Shrimpton was appointed manager. But he didn't last long. In 1852 he resigned, and, horror of horrors, he 'was superseded in the management by Mr Charles Baylis, of Redditch'. Ten years later Kirby, Beard & Company moved their whole operation to Redditch and that, to all intents and purposes, was the end of the industrial career of Long Crendon.

There was the usual lingering death, and one factory was reported still in existence when the *Victoria County History* was published in 1909, and it is said locally that manufacture on a small scale was still being carried on as late as 1927. But Kelly's Directory last enters a needlemaker at Long Crendon in 1895, when one Matthew Shrimpton was making sail needles.

William, of course, has clear and vigorous ideas as to the causes of the decline, and he may be right. But what is perhaps a more puzzling question is why the industry survived at Long Crendon as long as it did. With no advantages of raw material supplies, transport or proximity to markets it nevertheless held its own against rivals more favourably placed in almost every respect. The high value-added factor, of course lessens the advantages enjoyed by other manufacturers, but does not eliminate them. As with many other industries, it was the advent of steam power, with its appetite for cheap coal, that sounded the final knell, and perhaps the masters of Long Crendon were not so short-sighted as William thought them, to cling on to cheap, human motive power as long as they could. To have to haul coal ten or a dozen miles by four-horse dray from Aylesbury or Oxford, themselves many miles from the coal fields, must have been a horrible expense, and Kirby, Beard & Company no doubt quickly realised what a mistake they had made.

William's explanations, however, are more robust than these, and certainly more entertaining. Over-confidence is blamed. 'They clung with a childlike faith to the fact,' he says, 'that the good old trade names would never fail them, not even when breakers were ahead.' And an echo sounds in our ears as we read of these confident, hearty masters who 'preferred playing the clarionet, and joking with the farmers', and so 'made very little provision for increasing the trade of the village, nearly all of them being given to following the various sports and pastimes which were then held. . . .'

Perhaps it was worth it, after all.

MAX DAVIES
The Needlemakers of Long Crendon, 1970

Greater Celandine grows in Oving Churchyard and road verge. Graveyards, where the earth is clean and disturbed, are conducive to the growth of colonies of this plant, which does not like the closed shop so quickly established by the usual community of plants. The juice of the Greater Celandine is a Buckinghamshire cure for warts.

SUSAN COWDY
1971

It is the hedge, I think, which is the most truly English. Other countries can produce fields, a wealth of trees beside which our own appear often very ordinary. But no other country can produce anything which, like stitchery, binds together the varying pattern of the landscape in such a way that the pattern is made infinitely more beautiful.

If this seems extravagant, try to consider the English landscape without the hedge. It would not be the English landscape. The abolition of the common field system no doubt robbed the poor, a century or so ago, of many dearly held privileges; but in the quick hedge it bestowed a common glory on all of us.

. . . In the same way the Enclosure Acts, benefiting the rich, bestowed on us the most beautiful common inheritance, next to grass, that the English possess. Without the hedge we should all be poorer. I was brought up in a district notable for its lack of trees, but magnificent hedges. Without these hedges, huge lines of hawthorn umbrellas, making shade for cattle, that countryside would have been unbearably dull. Nothing else could have made it so beautiful in May-time, when the cream of the hawthorn bloom rose on the

An example of cut-and-laid hedging.

four sides of every field, making the air over-faint with scent. Nothing else could have created so happily the first rich drowsy feeling of summer.

In the south I have become acquainted with an entirely different hedge. In the Midlands the commonest hedge is undoubtedly the plain straight-set quick. Time has embroidered it with wild rose and blackberry, occasional ash-seedlings, bits of maple, but the quick remains indomitable. In the south, hedges are far more varied; quick is merely one colour, and no longer the common colour, in the pattern. If I walk out of my house I come straightway on a hedge which reads like a catalogue of shrubs: holly, dwarf oak, elder, maple, willow, wild-cherry, spindle, hazel, wild-rose, sallow, honeysuckle, blackberry, wild-clematis, blackthorn and always binding it together, hawthorn.

Along other lanes I shall see other variations: ash, sweet chestnut, vibur-

63

num, dogwood, crabapple, alder. There is scarcely any end to the variations of the south country hedge. This means that it is a thing of constant fascination throughout the twelve months of the year; in winter the comforting polished clumps of holly and their scarlet berries and the toy wooden balls of oak apples, in the very early spring the catkins of alder, the white stars of blackthorn, the emerald bread-and-cheese of hawthorn itself; in later spring the little odd trembling bouquets of wild cherry on coppery new leaves, the hawthorn bloom; in summer the glory of wild rose and elderbloom and honeysuckle, in autumn black and scarlet berries, nuts, the slit cerise and orange spindle seeds, old man's beard, acorns, the first bar winedipped dogwood, branches, the shining, comforting holly again.

But this is not all. This is only what the hedge is. It takes no account of what lives in or under it, or what flowers it shelters. In the Midlands we never expected a hedge to yield more than a patch of violets, a run of celandines, some pinky wild geraniums, late summer riots of willow herb in damp places. In the South every roadside hedge is a spring glory of primrose and bluebell, white anemones and violets, clouds of lady-smocks and campion; a summer tangle of foxglove and meadowsweet, wild canterbury bell and bay willow-herb, a hunting-place for wild strawberries.

The hedge, beginning as a simple device for the division of land, has become the haven sheltering every sort of flower and weed that pasturing and the plough drive out. Taken for twelve months of the year, in fact, the southern hedgerow is the most constant of all sources of satisfaction in the landscape. Yet even it, I think, reaches its glory at the flowering season of its commonest flower. When the kex is in bloom the hedge is etherealised. The light dense cloud of creamy flower lace, smothering the hedge itself, lifts it from earth. I can't remember any writer pausing to pay proper tribute to the kex, humblest of all flowers, rabbit-feed when young, make-believe lace in the games of little girls when in blossom, superb material for the whistles and pea-shooters of small boys at the height of summer. It is one of the things like the hedge itself which we take for granted. Yet I never see it now without marvelling at its effect of lace-light foam. It is something whipped airily out of the milk of springs.

H. E. BATES
'Hedge Chequerwork'
The Face of England, 1939

In every conversation we have held with different gentlemen in the several parts of the county, on the subject of inclosures, they have uniformly given it as their opinion, that the advantages already derived, and consequently still to be derived by inclosures, are an addition of rent to the landlord, an increase of produce to the farmer, in quantity and quality, and an improvement on the face of the soil, by draining, etc. It affords also shelter to the crops and cattle, and security to the farmer against the bad husbandry of his neighbour; but perhaps as material a consideration as any may be, that it gives to the farmer the liberty to manage his land in such a way as he finds most convenient without paying regard to what may be the practice of his neighbour.

We might ask, what would have been the state of agriculture throughout this kingdom, at the present day, if nothing but open fields were to be found? How inadequate would be the quality of grain produced, to the support of the present population, if two crops and a fallow was the custom throughout every parish? And which way would the middling class of people have derived any fuel in the interior parts of the kingdom, at a distance from peat and woodlands, and the farmer so many useful materials for agricultural purposes, if no inclosures by hedges, and trees in the hedge-rows, had ever taken place? Let any one consider these things seriously, and the conclusion will be unavoidable. If agriculture has attained to its present height through the means of inclosures (for with these the common fields are no where to be compared) it follows, that the more we inclose the more general will be the improvements.

WILLIAM JAMES AND JACOB MALCOLM
'Inclosing, and Its Advantages'
General View of Agriculture in Bucks, 1794

Chester Wilmot, 1911–1954, noted author and commentator, who resided in Cuddington, was war-correspondent for the BBC in western Europe, Special War-Correspondent during the Nuremburg trials; military correspondent for the *Observer*. Among his many books was *The Struggle For Europe*, published in 1952.

The annals of the steeplechase proper seem to commence in the year 1834, when the first important event of acknowledged record came off at St Albans where the renowned horses, Moonraker and Grimaldi, made so great a sensation. St Albans can boast of having provided the course for the first great public steeplechase, but I have always held that Aylesbury had the right to second honours.

One evening at the celebrated 'Crockfords' Club, discussing the peculiarities of the various hunting districts of England, Mr Henry Peyton, the eldest son of that 'prince of whips', Sir Henry Peyton – whose yellow drag and faultless team of greys with their brightly kept brass harness, with 'Old George' his esteemed stud groom, and Joe Buswell his second man 'perched up aloft' behind him, were a thing of renown in the 'Good Old Times' – spoke of the difficulties of crossing the Vale of Aylesbury, mentioning especially the brooks which intersected the course afterwards selected. This was questioned by some of the noble sportsmen present, and the conversation ended by a promise from Mr Peyton that he would undertake to give them a fair four-mile course over a hunting country which he himself had often ridden, and which he stated that men hunting in that district were compelled to face if they rode fairly to hounds like sportsmen. It should be noted that at that time Mr Peyton was allowed to be one of the best cross-country riders in England. His proposal was accepted, and he determined to carry it out.

He consulted his friend, Captain Lamb, on the subject, and the latter undertook to find a silver cup of fifty guineas as a prize, and the following conditions were drawn up and agreed to – each horse to carry 12 st. 7 lb., twenty guineas entrance P.P., the second horse to save his stake; and the race was fixed to come off within one month. When the entries were closed, it was found that there were twenty-one horses entered.

On the night before the race the headquarters of the committee, the White Hart at Aylesbury, was crowded with the élite of the sporting world; every inn was filled, and stables were at a premium. There was no railway then to the town, and as the race was timed for twelve o'clock there was but little chance of visitors from London arriving in time unless they came overnight. The course determined on was from Waddesdon windmill, about four and a half miles from Aylesbury, to a field in front of the church, the steeple of which forms a distinctive feature in the district and for some miles around. There is a small grass enclosure in front of the windmill, and the whole line, excepting about three acres of allotment and gardens near the town, was then under grass. The fences were left in their natural state, untrimmed, and were not only formidable in aspect, but really difficult to negotiate. The course was most severe, and comprised several doubles and tall bullfinchers, ox fences with post and rails, big singles, one cross-road, one deeply-rutted lane, one fairly-sized brook, one thick spinney, and the river Thame, about twenty-eight feet wide! This line ran parallel with the turnpike road, so that a horseman riding along it was able to keep abreast of the runners, and could see nearly every fence jumped. No flags marked the course, and until the morning of the race the line of country was kept a profound secret, for fear that any of the proposed riders should avail himself of the opportunity of seeing the fences and thus find out any weak place in the obstacles to be encountered.

On the morning of the race the company thronged the whole line of the turnpike road. The course to be taken was announced for the first time, but no flags whatever were used except the usual two in the winning-field. The horses, with their riders mounted, left the White Hart and other inns, after weighing in the yard of the headquarters. The colours worn by the riders were of unusual brilliance, and my memory enables me to recollect a trivial incident, which I remember telling to the late Lady Brassey, celebrated for her 'Voyage in the Sunbeam'. Whilst weighing, Mr Allnutt, Lady Brassey's father, appeared in a very resplendent satin jacket of purple and green plaid,

The Vale of Aylesbury Hunt at Chalgrove.

and Mr Peyton stroked it and said, 'How pretty. I wonder if it will be as clean as now at the end of the race.' Lady Brassey told me that she had that very jacket at home, and that her father had always treasured it as a memorable record of that great race.

This race was the prelude to many more in the Aylesbury Vale, and in the year 1836 two of the most celebrated steeplechases of the day were run during the February meeting of the Royal Hunt. The first was a heavyweight race, for horses carrying 12 st. 7 lb., and was run early in the day, on Tuesday, so that the hounds could meet after the conclusion of the race.

The fame of the Aylesbury Vale country, both as a hunting and steeplechasing centre, became now firmly established. The races usually took place about eleven o'clock, and the turn-out of the stag about half-past twelve, and after a jovial club dinner in the evening, the company were generally well tired out; but still it left time for many a joke and a freak. On one occasion the Marquis of Waterford brought his horse upstairs into the dining-room. Lord Jocelyn and Mr Ricardo led the horse up the garden steps, which were very steep indeed, took him into the dining-room and round the table, gave him some apples and biscuits, which he ate, and then commenced to get him downstairs. It was useless to attempt his descent by the same stairs, so steep were they, so he was led round the corridor to the front staircase, which was easy of descent. The floor of the passage was polished oak, and, although carpeted in the middle, the horse slipped badly, and at the head of the stairs obstinately refused to move one jot. At last he began kicking, smashed the passage windows, and soon cleared a ring behind him! Lord Jocelyn and his comrade resolutely sticking to his head. Eventually when a little quieted they blindfolded him and, once he began to descend, he could not stop, and blundered down into the entrance hall, having done himself no injury; and excepting to a few banisters and the smashing of some windows, but little damage was done.

J. F. K. FOWLER
Echoes of Old County Life, 1892

On 9th September 1852, the usually quiet village of North Marston was thronged with hundreds of excited people, all trying to get as close to the church as possible. They had gathered from far and near to witness the funeral of John Camden Nield, Esq., Barrister-at-law, who had been a familiar if eccentric figure in the neighbourhood for many years.

... John Camden Nield had died in London on 30th August, and – apart from a few meagre legacies – had left his entire fortune of £250,000, to Queen Victoria! This was an enormous sum, and the sensation was nation-wide.

Son of a prosperous London goldsmith who had devoted a great part of his time and wealth to charitable works and prison reform, Nield had in his youth enjoyed all the advantages money could provide. From Eton he went to Cambridge and there graduated first as a B.A., and later as an M.A. Passing on to Lincoln's Inn, he was called to the Bar in 1808 at the age of twenty-six. When his father, former High Sheriff of Buckinghamshire and magistrate for several other counties, died in 1814 – John, his only surviving child, inherited a large fortune. It included considerable property in Buckinghamshire.

The charitable paternal example had been in vain; John proved himself from the first a miser and an eccentric. The last thirty years of his life were devoted entirely to amassing money and expending just as little as possible.

In London he resided in a large house in Cheyne Walk. Apart from his housekeeper and a maid, his sole companion was a cat which was with him when he died. The house was meanly furnished – indeed, he is believed to have had no bed! When absent from town he put his housekeeper on the lowest board wages, and no mention was made of her in his will, although she served him for almost thirty years.

Twice a year Nield journeyed to Buckinghamshire to collect the rents of his scattered properties there. On those occasions he would stay with his tenants to avoid expense. In North Marston he always housed with the Neales at Rectory Farm. Once while there he attempted suicide because of a depreciation in one of his investments. Mrs Neale was able to save him.

Clad summer and winter in an old blue swallow-tailed coat with gilt buttons, brown trousers, short gaiters and much-patched shoes, he invariably carried a cotton umbrella green with age. He never wore a greatcoat, however severe the weather. That would have been an unheard-of extravagance. For fear it might cause his clothes to wear out, he would never permit them to be brushed. In contemporary accounts we read that wherever he stayed the compassionate housewife mended his rags as he slept!

For long distances he travelled by public conveyances – but always outside because it cost less. At other times this wealthy niggard made his way on foot to properties in remote situations. Not averse to accepting a lift however lowly and dirty, he never failed to reward the driver, although his ideas of remuneration were far from princely. Kind-hearted travellers often mistook him for an impoverished gentleman, and would send him refreshments. Such offerings were gratefully and politely received.

Nield usually refused to contribute to anything – but unlike other notorious misers – he broke this rule on a few occasions. Once he gave £1 to the Sunday School at North Marston, and several towards building a school at Aston Clinton. Other surprising donations were £50 to a training college at Culham, and an annual contribution to the Blind Asylum in London. After promising £300 towards an infirmary for Buckinghamshire, he withdrew the offer, disapproving of the site. Considering the son of a poor tenant unusually intelligent, he is believed to have financed at least part of his studies. The boy was Henry Tattam, who later became an eminent divine and Archdeacon of Bedford.

Queen Victoria accepted the fortune. She increased the bequests to each of the three executors from £100 to £1,000, made provision for Nield's faithful housekeeper and settled an annuity on Mrs Neale. Three years later she restored the chancel of North Marston church where the grave lies, contributed an East window with fine stained glass, and presented a reredos of sculptured Caen stone – all in memory of her benefactor.

The rest of the legacy was used to purchase the Balmoral estate.

ANNE CRAIG HOWIE
'A Victorian Sensation',
Bucks Life, May 1967

The method of deciding ownership, after the meadow was plotted out, was by drawing lots. This was done by cutting up a common dockweed into the required number of pieces to represent the lots, a well-understood sign being carved on each piece, representing crow's feet, hog's trough, and so on; these were placed in a hat and shaken up. Before this could be done, however, notice must be given by one of the men calling out at the top of his voice, 'Harko', and using some sort of wrigmarole, calling people to witness that the lots were drawn fairly and without favour. Long Crendon men working at Notley Abbey (just opposite Anxey), used to be highly amused

Renewing thatch on a cottage at Quainton.

with this custom, and the word 'harko' was echoed back with remarkable power, not only then but for weeks afterwards. The hat being shaken up, and one of the boys standing by, looking on with the greatest interest, is pitched upon a disinterested person to draw lots; and each owner had to 'sup up' with the lot that fell to him.

G. L. GOMME
The Village Community, 1890

An absurd rivalry existed between Haddenham and adjacent villages; boys from which, having dared to enter, were encouraged to make a speedy exit by stone and mud thrown by the Haddenham boys. Needless to write, retaliation was made when the position was reversed.

To this rivalry and previous lack of intercommunication, we may attribute foolish gibes orally handed down from far beyond the memory of man. Haddenham was labelled 'silly', and its folk credited with thatching its ponds in order to keep the ducks dry; also with looking at its surface to ascertain if it rained. Likewise it was reputed that the Long Crendon folk placed hurdles across the road to prevent the smallpox entering from Thame. Towersey folk were called 'gollings', possibly due to the fact that geese were prevalent there. But to which village belongs the credit of attempting to rake the reflection of the moon from a pond, under the impression that it was a cheese, the writer has never been able to ascertain.

All such denote the limited circle in which communities lived and moved, with the consequent narrow outlook on life.

Rivalry also existed between different parts of the village, and miserable petty fights were put up and encouraged amongst the boys. Taunts and challenges to fight were made and renewed until accepted; a group of excited youths ranging round the opponents with shrieks of encouragement and derision.

Thoughtless barbarism was also rife, a favourite youthful pastime being the stoning of birds in the hedges, called 'bird-wopping'. Boys, plentifully supplied with stones, lined the hedge on either side and chased the baffled bird to and fro until successful in killing it with a stone.

The arrival of the bicycle speedily reduced this spirit of uncouth villagism, its introduction providing ardent youth with means whereby they obtained a wider knowledge of life and conduct. The principle on which it was possible for a two-wheel, self-propelled machine to successfully run without falling down, was a much-discussed problem in the village, the writer's grandfather admitting that it passed his comprehension.

Its first appearance at Haddenham was in the form of the 'velocipede' – commonly and truly called 'boneshaker' – a two-wheel machine of wood and iron construction, with wheels of equal size and propelled by pedals on each end of the front wheel axle. Two enterprising brothers, Frederick and Joseph Ward, general smiths to the village, immediately rose to the occasion and obtained two of the said machines, which they hired to the village youths at threepence or fourpence per hour. Many were the hilarious, jolting rides enjoyed by the writer when a boy, over the rough roads of that period, and many the tumbles he experienced without serious injury.

On the track of the velocipede came the high bicycle now called 'penny-farthing', and the establishment of 'Ward Brothers' speedily became the convergent centre of interest for the district. It was the first appearance of a cycle made entirely of steel, and with rubber tyres; its lightness of construction was deservedly a marvel of interest, its graceful and noiseless speed evoked admiration not unmingled with awe.

Its popularity was immediate. Tailors, rising to the situation, produced specially made cycling suits, and many young men of the village, attired in knee-breeches and Norfolk coat, toured the district throughout the summer months. Objection to their speed and noiselessness of approach was raised by the elders; this, later on, was met by Act of Parliament enforcing bells and lights after sunset.

Turning back the mental pages of fifty years of continuous progress, the vision re-arises of the gloaming of a long summer's day: the peaceful benedictory hush and fragrant commingled scents of its dewy eve: the almost silent oncoming of the high cycles, their bright lamps swinging amid the flashing spokes of the large wheels, their riders sounding varied and melodious notes on the gongs as they passed swiftly by . . .

During the early evolution of the bicycle many amusing types were invented; many of them the products of local craftsmen. A wooden and iron construction ran about the village, on which the rider sat astride the front wheel, with two wheels about two-thirds its size following behind. Between the said wheels was an iron crate arrangement – large enough for a child to sit within – for the conveyance of luggage. It is said that extraordinary strength was required to propel it. Another 'penny-farthing' type had levers and cranks that worked the front axle, the object being to allow the rider to sit farther back and nearer the ground. . . .

The tricycle made many brave bids for favour, and many types of construction appeared, the most singular being one with a large driving wheel to the left-hand side, with two smaller wheels running alongside to the right. For a long time there existed a natural belief that the two-wheel cycle was, of necessity, more dangerous than one with more, and it required several years of experience to prove that a spill on the latter was equally likely, and worse than the former.

Although vastly improved from their previous condition, the roads of that period – in comparison with now – were still very bad. Stones picked from the fields, and flints carted off the hills, were used for their repair. These were broken by old men, past work on the farms, and spread over the roads and allowed to remain there until ground in by passing carts. In winter-time long stretches of newly-stoned road were frequent, making progress even in horse and cart slow and difficult; in consequence of which many preferred walking to and from market, to the discomfort of a slow ride on a cold day. Dusty in summer and muddy in winter, the cycle rider had need ever to be wary of loose stones, ruts and puddles. The precarious balance of the high bicycle made selection of the best parts of the road essential. This was seldom appreciated by the old-time carter; thus the sudden meeting of a cart or wagon, or the uncertain movements of sheep and cattle, then frequent on the roads, oft-times caused a dilemma – the rider being forced to take the slanting margin, with the result that balance was upset and he would discover himself deposited on the road in front of the machine. But notwithstanding the almost inevitable cropper, athletic youth, then as now, gloried in the element of danger, and it was acknowledged that the old high bike deposited its burden with an ease and grace not known to any other order of construction.

WALTER ROSE
Fifty Years Ago, 1920

Thomas Bourdillon, 1924–1956, whose home was in Quainton, was a member of the British Expedition to Mount Everest in 1953.

When Napoleon the Great, at the beginning of this century, drove the Royal Family out of France, and they sought shelter with us, our Government were doubtful where they could be placed in safety, so as to prevent a *coup de main* either from the French themselves, or by the Revolutionary party in England; and it was deemed necessary for their security that the Royal exiles should reside somewhere in the centre of England. Hartwell was the place selected, a stately mansion surrounded with fine timber, standing in a park of great pastoral beauty. A picturesque little church, embosomed in trees is within a hundred yards of the mansion, with large kitchen gardens and remarkably pleasing ornamental grounds adjoining it, with shady alcoves enclosing a lovely bowling-green, where Louis XVIII and his small Court were fond of disporting themselves. About the year 1808 they took up their residence at Hartwell, and the resources of the little village were strained to their utmost to accommodate the Court. Every lodge, even the gardeners' and gamekeepers' cottages, were occupied by Royalties or important people attendant on the King. In one small cottage in the wood was housed the Duchesse d'Angoulême; the Duc de Berri in one of the lodges, in another the Duc de Blacas; whilst the King and his amiable consort, with the Prince de Condé, and their personal retinue, occupied the mansion, one of the rooms of which was fitted up as a chapel with confessional, and other rooms for the abbé attendant on his Majesty. The French nobility with their families, were to be seen visiting the primitive inhabitants of this Buckinghamshire village, and often extended their walks to attend the market at the town of Aylesbury, which stands about two miles distant.

In that town my father had come to reside, when about twenty-one years of age (in 1812) and wonderful to relate, had already acquired, at Berkhampstead Grammar School, a good knowledge of the French language – a rare accomplishment in those days, when the Continent was practically closed against all but the wealthiest Englishmen – and he was almost the only man in the neighbourhood of Aylesbury who could converse with the Royal Family and their retinue. The King often sent for him on matters of business, and I have heard him tell many anecdotes of the residents of the house, and of the habits there of the French Court. Generally the King, with a certain amount of royal state, dined in public, and people were admitted to walk past the party when at dinner. The French Queen died at Hartwell: after the entrance of the allies into Paris, in 1814, her body was taken to France, and I believe was buried at St Denis. Portraits of Louis XVIII, 'Louis le Désiré', as he was called, are still to be seen in Hartwell House, with Prince de Condé and other celebrities attached to the retinue of the King. The old churchyard has several memorials of those who died in exile, but I cannot find that any Frenchman or Frenchwoman remained behind when the King for the last time left the village. I have many times in wandering among the shady groves of Hartwell found, carved on the trees, lines giving expression to the sense of comfort and happiness which the exiles experienced during their prolonged stay here; one tree has carved deeply in the bark, 'Quel Plaisir', another beech-tree, 'Toujours Heureux'.

Louis, on his return to France, had a garden formed and planted at Versailles, on the plan, exactly reproduced of the Queen's private garden at Hartwell, that he might commemorate, so he said, 'the happy days he had spent in that charming county'. This garden still exists, but very few of the visitors to the glorious palace of Versailles who ask for 'Le Jardin Anglais', are aware of its origin. During the past twenty years I have twice visited it, but am bound to say, that either the one has been so grown over, or the other at Hartwell has been so altered, that I failed to connect them, except in the general outline and usual character of a truly 'English' garden.

At Aylesbury great were the rejoicings in 1814 and loud shoutings when it was announced that the allied armies had entered Paris, that the great Napoleon had signed his abdication, and that 'the King would have his own again'. The town of Aylesbury was en fête as the French King passed through it on his way to London – a narrow street leading into the Market Square still perpetuates the memory of the event by bearing the name of Bourbon Street. My father with five other young men mounted their horses to form a small bodyguard and rode by the side of the King's carriage, intending to go as far as the first stage to Great Berkhampstead, about fourteen miles from Hartwell. The King's carriage was drawn by four post-horses, and several other carriages followed. On arriving at Berkhampstead the first change of horses was at the King's Arms, then kept by a Mr Page, who had three very good-looking daughters; one of them, sweet Miss Polly – not sweet Anne – Page, the King had often been much struck with; and he never passed through the town either going to or coming from the Metropolis without having a chat and paying attentions to 'sweet Polly Page'. This was well known to my father and his friends, and they knew therefore, that a quarter of an hour or so would be consumed in the ostensible act of changing horses, while the King would devote the time to a flirtation with the fair Polly. They therefore pushed on to Boxmoor, about four miles, gave their horses a mouthful of hay and some water, and waited for the King's arrival, intending to accompany him as far as Watford. His Majesty caught sight of the cavalcade, and expressed to my father the pleasure he felt at their attention. Being well mounted, they trotted on another seven miles to Watford, and there hearing that our Prince Regent, with many of the great officers of State, and several Royal princes from the Continent, were assembled to meet his Majesty at Stanmore, they resolved, if possible, to see their historic interview. Riding on to Bushey, without stopping at Watford, they had time to have their somewhat tired horses groomed down and fed, and by the time the King arrived, four of them, for two could not get further than Boxmoor – were mounted and ready again to continue their escort; and they thus rode on to the Abercorn Arms at Stanmore. There was a great crowd around the portico of the inn, and a guard of cavalry to receive his Majesty. My father and his three friends

Hartwell House, now a private secretarial and liberal-arts college for girls, dates from 1600, but the south front was added by Henry Keene in the eighteenth century. The house was once owned by the Hampden family; early in the seventeenth century it passed to the Lees. From 1809 to 1814 it was the residence of Louis XVIII and his Court during their period of exile. The garden, which is one of the great attractions of the estate, was laid out by 'Capability' Brown, and includes a lake with a stone bridge, part of which was fashioned from the old central arch of Kew Bridge.

pushing forward, the King seemed greatly pleased, and desired them to keep near him. They jumped off their horses and stood on each side of the entrance, and saw the Prince Regent embrace the French King, and receive him with much affection amidst the enthusiasm of the people, which was unbounded. Again mounting their nags, they rode towards London; within about a mile from London the Royal cortège again overtook them, and they accompanied the King to the Pulteney Hotel (I think that was the name) where his retinue were to be accommodated. After seeing the King safely bestowed, my father and his friends rode off, tired enough, to the Old Bell in Holborn, at that time one of the leading inns in London, and which may yet be seen in its primitive state, the galleries round the old stable-yard, the old coffee-room, with box divisions, scarcely altered for one hundred and fifty years or more.

J. F. K. FOWLER
Echoes of Old County Life, 1892

The first Vale of Aylesbury Steeplechase, 1835. From paintings by F. C. Turner.

Above, top: A correct view near Blackgrove Farm where the horses met, having at an early part of the Chase taken different directions.

Above: Fleet Marston Brook with the Chapel in the distance.

Right, above: Mr Simpson's Berryfield Farm, Ivy Ground.

Right, below: Mr Joseph Terry's Long Furlong Field, the Red Flag forming the winning post.

Article I. Every man shall present himself at the place of meeting quietly, suitably clothed, and in good time. He who rides his hunter steadily thereto is better than he who uses a hack. He who drives tandem for display or who uses any manner of engine or machine, except as a necessity, is an abomination.

Article II. Every man shall first salute and speak words of comfort to the huntsman and whippers-in, knowing full well that they have hard work to perform. He shall then count the hounds and examine them with great joy, but in a quiet manner. He shall then likewise cheerfully salute his friends. He that shall say that the day will be a bad-scenting one, or in any manner

77

endeavour to prophesy evil, is an abomination.

Article III. It is acceptable that those of experience shall, at all times, give explanation and encouragement by word and deed to all young persons, so that fox-hunting may continue in the land from generation to generation. He who thinks he knows, when he knows not, is an abomination.

Article IV. Every man shall remember that the ground he passes over is not his own property. Whosoever uses not due care and consideration is an abomination.

Article V. He who talks loudly or who leaps unnecessarily is an abomination. He who wears an apron or mackintosh on wet days or who uses any other device for making a mountebank of himself, or who in any way causes inconvenience to any hound or hunt servant is an abomination.

Article VI. If it be possible, let every true believer abstain from all meat and drink, save only such as is necessary to sustain life. Let the whole day be kept as a special fasting and strengthening of mind for the Chase. In the evening he shall partake of suitable meat and drink, and on the evening after a good day he shall have a special allowance.

Article VII. He who of his own free will, goes home before the hounds do, or who is displeased with the day, or who is not fully uplifted, joyful and thankful because of the day, is an abomination.

Article VIII. Whosoever kills or takes a fox by any other means save by hunting is an abomination; may his dwelling become desolate and his possessions a desert; may his mind be filled with bitterness and his body with pain.

Article IX. Whosoever lives a cheerful, good neighbour, striving to help and encourage his friends at all times, and who hunts on foot if he has not a horse, and by whose behaviour the Scarlet is never brought into dishonour; may he live long and be happy and may his possessions be as the sand by the seashore for multitude.

Article X. And may all men, rich and poor, have equal rights and pleasures in the Chase if they devoutly agree to these articles.

WILLIAM FAWCETT
'The Ten Commandments of Hunting',
in *The Old Berkeley Beagles*, 1939

Anybody who wanted to show a visitor from overseas the wildlife of a typical stretch of English countryside could do no better than to drive to any village near Aylesbury, leave the car and walk along one of the many footpaths which lead out over the fields.

The large area of farmland is well studded with woods, and criss-crossed with hedgerows, an important wildlife habitat which is rapidly being eradicated in parts of the eastern counties and elsewhere. The Vale would no

Saved from demolition and bought from the demolition contractors by Wing Commander and Mrs Patrick Brunner, Wotton House was built by Richard Grenville in 1704, using the same plan that Sheffield, Duke of Buckingham, used for Buckingham House, later to become known as Buckingham Palace. The ornamental stonework was fashioned by Grinling Gibbons; the wrought-iron balustrade on the staircase by Tijou; the gates, screen and voir-claire by Robinson. The landscaping was 'Capability' Brown's first job on his own. In 1820 a fire gutted the interior, and the Marquis of Buckingham called upon his friend, Sir John Soane, to undertake the restoration. Subsequent restoration by the Brunners in 1957 has in all details been faithful to Soane's plans which fortunately have been preserved in the Soane Museum. The house is flanked by two pavilions, one of which is owned by Sir Arthur Bryant.

longer be the Vale if it were deprived of the hedges where whitethroats and yellowhammers sing every summer; where hawthorn, crab and blackthorn blow every spring, and where cow parsley, so prettily named Queen Anne's Lace, adorns the roadsides every year from late April to late May. The road verges are also one of the important habitats for wildlife which has been driven out elsewhere by intensive farming methods. Since most people now travel by car or coach, their impression of the English countryside and especially of its wildflowers is largely dependent on what they see nearest to them, on the roadsides. Co-operation between the local Naturalists' Trust and the County Surveyor has resulted in a compromise about methods of trimming verges so that only the few feet nearest the road are cut in the spring and summer in order to allow the many species of attractive and sometimes rare wild flowers to grow and seed.

The meadows in the Vale are yellow every spring with buttercups and, in some secluded pastures, with cowslips as well, later turning red with sorrel and sometimes almost white with moon daisies. Certain special meadows at Ford and Haddenham still hold a few flowers of the beautiful snakeshead fritillary, locally known as frog-cup or 'fraw-cup'. The second Sunday in May is still known as Frawcup Sunday when villagers go out to pick the few surviving blooms. This seems a great pity; with so few remaining the flowers should be left for others to enjoy. In the summer of 1971, Friends of the Vale, together with representatives of the Berkshire, Buckinghamshire and Oxfordshire Naturalists' Trust and the Nature Conservancy, sowed fritillary seeds from Magdalen meadows in two water meadows at Notley Abbey. The site will be scientifically managed in co-operation with the owner, in hopes that in a few years flowers will appear. Here Frawcup Sunday will be celebrated with cameras, not by picking.

Elsewhere in the Vale damp meadows contain most interesting breeding birds. Along the river Thame between Haddenham and Long Crendon both curlews and yellow wagtails breed, and in the pollard willows are redstarts with their handsome fiery tails. Curlews, together with redshanks, also breed in the wet meadows of the Grendon Underwood region.

Chalk grassland is a speciality of the Chilterns rather than the Vale, but at Cheddington are two low hills, outcrops of the Chilterns, where an old chalk pit has been established as a BBONT reserve containing a fine display of chalk plants from May to early September; notably the Chiltern gentian, a magnificent large relative of the common autumn gentian or felwort, and the clustered bellflower. Lime-loving plants also grow in other parts of the Vale, such as bee orchids on the railway embankment near Chearsley. The butterfly orchid, which likes lime but also grows on neutral soils, can be found at Waddesdon Manor. Here the Naturalists' Trust have advised on the management of the grassland, so that it is not mown until the orchids have finished blooming. A fine colony of marsh orchids can be found along the Thame, near Nether Winchendon.

Of the many fine woods in the Vale, it seems invidious to choose any for special mention, but Rushbeds and the nearby woodlands of Grendon Underwood, Doddershall and Claydon cannot be passed by. These are relics of the ancient Bernwood Forest which lay along the western perimeter of the Vale through Boarstall and the Shabbington woods to Waterperry. Here grew fine oaks with an under storey of hazel and blackthorn. In recent years much of the oak has been felled and replaced with conifers; however, there are still some areas where examples of the old oak forest remain. Rushbeds, once a superb lowland oak wood, will soon become a BBONT reserve. It is especially rich in woodland butterflies, and contains spotted orchids, golden saxifrage and pendulous sedge, among countless other plants. Nightingales breed here, as they do in many other sequestered woods and copses of the Vale.

Wotton Lakes and their environs hold a wide variety of wild life, including butterfly and marsh orchids, and the rare fly honeysuckle, though this was probably planted. Here many woodland birds breed. Some, such as the lesser spotted woodpecker and stock dove, taking advantage of the dead trees which fortunately have not been felled, in which nest-holes of all shapes and sizes occur. The large reed beds provide a home for the summer-visiting reed warbler, not a common bird in the Vale, while in the winter vast numbers of starlings roost in the dead reeds, taking shelter from the wind. In some years the hobby breeds, choosing perhaps the abandoned nest of a crow in a tall tree overlooking undisturbed fields.

The woods at Grendon Underwood hold the finest areas of primroses and cowslips in the county. Muntjac, or barking deer, which originated in China but actually escaped many years ago from Woburn across the Bedfordshire border, breed in these wet oak-hazel woods. In the woodlands around Boarstall Decoy early spring brings that remarkable little greenish flower moschatel, known as 'town-hall clock' from the fact that its four or five flowers face away from each other on a cube, like the clock faces on so many Victorian town halls.

The Vale is not as rich in water habitats as some other parts of the country; the important wildfowl refuges of Tring Reservoirs, a national nature reserve, and Foxcote Reservoir, a wildlife refuge held by the County Trust, lie just beyond its limits. It does, however, contain Boarstall Decoy, maintained by the Wildfowlers' Association who have set up their conservation headquarters here; the fine lakes at Wotton Underwood, and the important flooded brick pits at Calvert. Some 300 ducks, including wigeon, goldeneye, gadwall and pochard, spend the winter there, and great crested grebes, dabchicks and reed warblers breed there as well. Large numbers of gulls frequent the rubbish dumps alongside the pits, leaving each winter evening to roost on the London reservoirs some fifty miles away. Alas, these pits are now threatened: a sailing club is using one, thus driving the wildfowl away; whilst draining to make room for yet more rubbish may eliminate the other. The reservoir at Weston Turville has long been famous for its bird life; here there are a fishing and a sailing club, while the banks and reed beds (and shooting rights) are leased by the County Trust as a nature reserve.

When man moves in, wildlife moves out. This is why it is vital that certain sites be maintained for the animals and flowers which give the Vale its distinctive character. RICHARD FITTER AND SUSAN COWDY
March 1972

The Buckinghamshire Swan, reproduced from a drawing in the possession of the Buckinghamshire Archaeological Society.

We have settlers in the garden;
they came, and stayed, left Afric heat
because the Chilterns suits them well,
and saves them flying all that way!
We did not ask the doves – they came,
at first a pair, searching vainly,
doubtful to build, because the trees
were not of the kind they knew.
At last they chose an ancient plum,
quickly made a nest, discarded
it to try once more elsewhere
in the untidy orchard.
This year the couples multiplied –
house-bound, for they cling to humans,
but slowly, surely they increase,
and we waken to their call.
Now when Autumn lights the bonfire,
(the rubbish-heap of leaves has grown),
we hear them jostle, see them fly,
dipping wings to fan the flame.

RUTH REYNOLDS
Collared Doves, 1972

Some attempt has been made to compile a list of Bucks dialect words; most of those which follow appear there, though not all. The present endeavour is merely to place on record a few words which may often be heard in the Vale of Aylesbury in 1922.

Often the word is a mere variation of an ordinary dictionary word, though possibly with a slight variation in meaning. For example:

ATHIRT: from 'athwart' or 'across'; 'Ar, come athirt the gardin.'
BLATE: 'A blatin' cow soons forgets her calf.' Here the word is clearly a variant of 'bleat'.
BUNT: to butt, as sheep attack with lowered head.
CLA'HOLT: to claw or catch hold of anything.
FOTCH: the past tense of 'fetch'.
KID: a pod, used as a verb: 'These pays have kidded well.' Possibly it is a variant of 'cod'.
KURLICK: a mere corruption of 'charlock' or wild mustard.
LATTERN: late, particularly of fruit ripening after the bulk of the crop.
OKKARD: awkward, in the sense of 'obstinate'.

More interesting, because less obvious, are the following words:

'ACCLE: 'accle yoursel', meaning 'hurry up!'

'AGGLE: to vex. 'I wor fair aggled.' The original meaning seems to be 'soil, or defile', as in bad weather, consequently the annoyance proceeding from this untidyness, or from any other source of discomfort or irritation. (Query: Is it cognate with 'draggle'?)

BRANSINGS: a corruption of 'brands' ends', or the pieces which drop from the fire-dogs when a log has burnt through in the middle.

DILLING: the smallest pig in the litter, said to be a corruption of 'darling'. If so it is certainly not mother's darling, because the least of a litter of pigs has less than its due share of milk, being squeezed out.

GARM: to smear: 'E wor all garmed up wi' mud.'

GLIBBY: Slippery, used of the roads in frosty weather. The word is spelt 'gliddy' in Wright, and he explains it as akin to 'glide', but it seems to the present writer to have a 'b' sound.

HARRUP: to scratch or dig.

OVER-RIGHT: opposite, 'Ye'll see 'im over-right t' wood-geeate.'

PIMMOCKY: dainty, said by Mr Cocks to mean 'slightly unwell, indisposed', but it indicates rather a fanciful choice of an invalid or spoiled child.

PITCHING: the stone or brick-paved yard, on which milk-cans can be drained, etc.

SHUT IN (OR OUT): to harness or unharness – the phrase is invariably used. Not wishing to stop long on a visit, one says: 'I won't shut out, thank 'ee.'

SLOMMAKIN': slatternly, slovenly.

UNKID: strange, unusual, nasty, ugly, dreary, etc. Halliwell derives it from A.S. un-cwyd=quiet, solitary; while Wright compares it with uncouth. It is often used adverbially; 'Ar were unkid frit,' meaning 'I was uncommonly frightened.'

WATSHUT: A corruption of wet-shod. Thus, the present writer having walked through Grendon Wood in winter was greeted with the exclamation: 'Then ar'll warr'nt 'ees watshut.'

The unfortunate effect of a standardised educational curriculum, together with modern facilities of transport must be to do away with local words and phrases, and so help to destroy county character as much as a standardised house upsets the individuality of the native product. The present writer is among those who deplore this tendency, but he sees one distinct advantage in education, namely, the destruction of superstition in its more mischievous forms. He has never seen evidence of faith in spells or charms, and where ill-founded beliefs linger they are such as harm nobody. It is thought, for example, that in alternate years the pods of broad beans point upwards and downwards, and that the pips of apples in a similar way point to and from the core. There are often some fowls which roost in trees in preference to the henhouse. It is imagined that if a fox stands below them in the moonlight the reflected glare from his eyes has such an effect on the birds that they drop into his expectant mouth. There may be something more than superstition in the idea that the root of the wild arum ('lords and ladies') dried and chopped finely and then mixed with a horse's corn much improves the appearance of its coat.

A 'charm' for warts very recently practised successfully by a buxom young woman near Ashendon was as follows: 'I took an ould hoddy-snail and rubbed him on the wart, and then shoved a thorn through him and throwed him away where I told nobody.' The cure, though unkind to the snail, was efficacious.

On the whole it would seem that the men of Bucks are as vigorous mentally as they certainly are physically. An expression sometimes used of a healthy infant is: 'Aye, a's fierce and hale.' Such a child, one thinks, must have been . . . he (who) for years used to walk four miles to work each morning, and always passed Aylesbury Church when the clock was striking four. When he reached home in the evening he used to be glad of moonlit nights so that he could work in his allotment. But that is a feeble performance in comparison with a man named Lacey, who once lived at Princes Risborough; he was an under-sawyer, and was working one year at St Leonard's. Thither he walked each morning, and it could hardly be less than nine or ten miles. At night he used to walk back carrying one of the great outside 'slabs' or first cuts from the trunk, which are the sawyer's perquisite. The top-sawyer, who lived at or near Cholesbury, offered him the use of a room in his own cottage, to save him this tremendous walk, but Lacey indignantly answered: 'Stop here along o' you? I've my taters to mould up when I gets whoam.' Mr T. Bishop of College Farm, Aston Clinton, vouches for this story.

The mention of physical vigour reminds one of a story which is told of the late Mr Treadwell, of Upper Winchendon, the well-known sheep-breeder. He met the Rector of Waddesdon, who was about to marry, though somewhat late in life, and said to him: 'Is this right, Rector, that you're a-going to get married; I hopes not.' 'Really,' replied the reverend gentleman, 'Why should I not be married?' 'Well, I only hopes as she bain't a young wife.' 'Why?' said the Rector, 'the patriarchs married young wives, you know.' 'That may be, Rector, but you ha'n't got a patriarch's constitootion.'

They who have the wisdom to pass their lives in the country generally turn out 'good lives', in the Assurance Companies' meaning of the phrase. Thus a woman was found in a very depressed state one evening, mourning for her father who had died that morning 'in his eighty-eight'. 'He never had a day's illness afore the las' week or two, when he took to 'is bed, – but he wasted tarrible.'

'He was unable to eat, I suppose?' enquired her listener.

'It worn't that altogether; he ate a pretty fair dinner yesterday, 'awever, but he didn't eat much today . . . he died afore dinner time.'

It is wrestling with the stubborn earth which makes us strong, but when the land is *too* stiff it may almost win the contest. For instance, one of the last Duke of Buckingham's tenants at Wotton was named Cave; his land was low-lying and wet. He had just been through a bad time with his sheep, and he was feeling somewhat desperate. When he knew that the Duke was likely to be about he took care to meet him, but mounted on a bull. The Duke was naturally astonished, and asked him why he had taken to such a mount, receiving the reply: 'Well, your Grace, my land's that wet it's pulled the guts out o' my hosses, so I must either ride thishyer animal or take to a boat.'

This chapter may fittingly be closed with a mention of the common use of 'carr' for 'carry'. An old and much respected neighbour of the writer is in constant requisition as a bearer at funerals. Referring once to this he said: 'If there's as many to carr' me to the grave as I've carr'ed – I reckon the chu'chyard'll be proper full.'

G. ELAND
In Bucks, 1923

> The farmers of Aylesbury gathered to dine,
> And they ate their prime beef, and they drank their old wine,
> With the wine there was beer, with the beer there was bacca,
> The liquors went round and the banquet was crowned
> With some thundering news from the Straits of Malacca.
> Attributed to WILLIAM EWART GLADSTONE
> Nineteenth Century

Creslow, the smallest parish in the county, has, or had, the largest field: the 'great pasture' containing three-hundred-and-twenty-seven acres and a romantically-situated old house, now vastly altered, that once had a famous 'haunted room'. The surrounding Creslow pastures, long celebrated for their exceptional fertility, were once Crown property. Cattle and produce from these fields supplied the tables of the monarchs from Queen Elizabeth I to King Charles II. Creslow Manor House was originally built by the Knights Templars who acquired the land in 1120 and added to by the Knights Hospitallers of St John of Jerusalem. In succeeding years much has been destroyed and much added, notably the gabled Elizabethan octagonal turret and groined crypt or dungeon. The confiscation of monastic property during the reign of Henry VIII made Creslow pass to the Crown with more alterations. Some seventy years ago the chapel, once attached to the manor house, was a stable, and the farmyard formerly part of a graveyard. There is still Tudor panelling and plaster decorations in parts of the house which must have been even more picturesque, romantic and isolated among high trees a hundred years ago when its haunted room gained and held its reputation.

It was about 1850, it seems, that a former High Sheriff of Buckinghamshire visited Creslow to attend a dinner party. His house was some miles distant and as the weather turned stormy, he was pressed to stay the night – provided that he had no objection to sleeping in the haunted room. He said he was interested in the possibility of meeting a ghost, for he did not believe in the supernormal; being a strong and fit man, he was convinced that any practical joker would more than meet his match – should anyone think to 'play the ghost' that night.

Accordingly the room was prepared. He desired no fire or night-light, but took with him a box of matches so that he might light a candle if he wished to do so. He armed himself with a cutlass and a pair of pistols – amid much joking between himself and his host.

Morning came, clear and bright after the stormy night, and the other guests gathered round their host and hostess in the breakfast room. Someone remarked that the visitor who had slept in the haunted room was not present. A servant was dispatched to summon him but soon returned, saying that his repeated knocking had brought no answer and that a jug of water left outside the room an hour before, was still there. Two or three of the gentlemen went up to the chamber and after also knocking loudly several times, entered – to find the room empty! No servant had seen anything of the guest, but since he was a county magistrate, it was thought he had left early to attend a meeting. Then it was found that his horse was still in the stable; and so, at last, perplexed and a little worried, the guests sat down with their hosts to eat and were in the middle of their breakfast, when in walked the missing guest!

He had, he said, locked and bolted his room on entering it the night before, and then proceeded to examine carefully the whole place. Only when quite satisfied that no living creature but himself was in the room and that every entry was sealed did he go to bed, expecting to have a good night's rest. But shortly after dropping off to sleep he was awakened by the sound of light footsteps, accompanied by a rustling noise, like that of a silk gown. He got up quietly, lit a candle, and searched the room but could find nothing to account for the noise which had ceased as soon as his feet had touched the floor. He looked under the bed, in the fireplace, up the chimney and at both doors which were fastened and locked as he had left them. Glancing at his watch he found the time was a few minutes after midnight. Since all seemed quiet again, he returned to bed and was soon asleep. Then he was awakened again, by the same noises – but this time they were much louder: he heard the violent rustling of a stiff silk dress and distinct footsteps which told him, he thought, exactly where the figure was in the room. This time he sprang out of bed, darted to the spot where he felt the figure must be and tried to grasp the intruder in his arms. But his arms met and there was nothing there. The noise moved to another part of the room and he followed it, groping near the floor to prevent anything passing under his arms, but still he found nothing. Eventually the sounds died away at the doorway to the crypt, and the visitor returned to bed, leaving a lighted candle burning, but more than a little perplexed at being totally unable to detect the origin of the noise or account for its cessation when he lighted the candle.

Mr D. G. Hares told me in 1967 that the inside of the house had been extensively altered and no room remained as it once did; he had no personal knowledge of any ghost at Creslow.

PETER UNDERWOOD
Gazetteer of British Ghosts, 1971

The one characteristic that can be described as common to the churches of those fifty-odd parishes set down as belonging to the Vale of Aylesbury is that of variety. The same can be said of the whole county of Buckingham. Unlike the churches in other counties there is no common denominator of style, plan, group, material or feature – which of course is the secret of their charm: one never knows what one will discover next.

Some people complain of this lack of a common type or recognisable uniformity. Where are the great towers of Somerset? Where are the 'spires of the shires'? Where the vast (and monotonous) flint 'wool' churches of Norfolk and Suffolk, or the woodwork (roofs, screens, seating) of the West Country or East Anglia? The answer is that the Vale of Aylesbury provides examples of one or two or all of these things, but not in profusion, and not on a vast scale, so that what there is shines out from a modest background in the manner of small, refined jewels, and is not lost in a great regalia of splendour.

The reason for such variety is probably twofold: it may be partly due to the great disparity in wealth and influence of the various Lordships and Manors in the area. Chiefly, though, it is due to the wide range of building materials available. For of course, in times when roads were poor or non-existent, the transportation of heavy materials over long distances was a matter of great difficulty and expense. As a result, local builders used whatever sound material was ready to hand – clay for bricks and tiles, chalk and flint in parishes bordering the Chilterns, small stone rubble or poor oolite limestone to the north of the Vale, and finer limestone further to the north. That is why buildings in villages of the past seem to have 'grown' where they stand; indeed, they are really part of the landscape, roofed by straw thatch from the corn fields, timbered from the oaks and elms of the local woods, plastered and lime-washed from the local chalk, and coloured by ochre and umber. We may be thankful that in the Middle Ages there existed no concrete, no Fletton brick, no gypsum plasterboard or coke breeze blocks for universal transport and erection in an alien context. The contents of the churches themselves are just as varied and interesting, with monuments, brasses, carvings, fonts and other details of local interest in profusion.

With such a mixed bag it is difficult to know what to choose. But most probably one should begin with Aylesbury itself. The church is the largest in the county – a fine town church that crowns the low hill on which Aylesbury stands, and which formerly dominated the scene before certain modern intrusions upset the scale and balance. It is basically thirteenth century, with a central tower, transepts, chapels and a long chancel. It is somewhat disappointing in detail as it was too heavily restored in the nineteenth century, and has lost much of its texture. But it still retains the remarkable features of a central timber pillar to the south chapel, a twelfth-century font that gives the type-name to a group of a dozen or more similar ones in the neighbourhood, and a seventeenth-century monument to the Lee family of Quarrendon. A fresh red flower is still regularly placed on this monument, in accordance with a touching inscription.

Other cruciform churches of splendid proportion just within the Aylesbury area are those of Bierton and Long Crendon, the latter standing in a superb village above the Thame Valley.

Within the periphery of the Vale must be included two churches which are not only the finest of their type within the county, but also rank high in all of England. These, of course, are the churches of Wing and Stewkley. Wing, although one would never suppose it from the exterior, except for the polygonal apse, is a Saxon basilica of the seventh century, with a crypt altered by the Lady Elfgivu in the tenth century. It out-ranks Brixworth, for Brixworth has lost its aisles. Stewkley is a text-book Norman, three-cell building, hardly altered from the time it was built in the mid-twelfth century by the same patron (and probably by the same masons) as Cassington, rather earlier, near Oxford.

Deserted places have a romantic charm and mystery about them. The Vale area contains a number of such sites. The church of Fleet Marston, closed and forlorn, is declared redundant, and stands isolated in the middle of a deserted village. Quarrendon has long since vanished, though I can remember it as a boy, with the arcades still standing alongside the moats; lumps and bumps of a long-abandoned village, and a manor house in which Queen Elizabeth I was once entertained by the Lees. The village nucleus at Stoke Mandeville shifted, and the old church was abandoned, to be pulled down quite recently. And what, we wonder, happened at Cublington, where there is a castle mound and a cemetery site, presumably with a church on low ground, and a 'new' church higher up, where an early fifteenth-century brass commemorates the first incumbent?

The Kimbles are an interesting pair – one large and splendid (with an 'Aylesbury' font) and associated with John Hampden; the other small, humble, but beautiful, and containing, artistically, the best wall painting in Bucks; also, a set of 'Chertsey' tiles telling the story of the Arthurian legend – Lancelot and Guinevere and King Mark – a strange thing to find in a village church.

Hulcott and Aston Abbots are typical small but interesting churches of the low-lying country of the Vale. But if you go a little further afield to the edge of the rising ground west and north-west of Aylesbury itself, you will find such places as Quainton and Hardwick. At Quainton is a splendid group consisting of church, almshouses and rectory, and probably the finest series of monuments in the whole area, including one to the Winwood family, founder of the almshouses; and a superb and touching memorial, possibly by Roubilliac to Justice Dormer (1728–30) and his son; others to John and Fleetwood Dormer by William Stanton, and a Leoni to Sir Richard Piggot.

Nearly all the other Vale churches contain at least one item of rarity or interest; for example, Dinton (neglected and stripped of its plaster) with its splendid Norman south doorway and tympanum containing a Latin hexameter inscription on the impost. Or Stone, with a rare Norman font that came originally from Hampstead Norris in Berkshire and has carvings associated with the Hercules legend. Or Cuddington with a most unusual building development representing three or four changes actually within the thirteenth century. Or Ellesborough, Chilton and Waddesdon, each with a splendid monument of different dates.

Perhaps the Winchendons, Upper and Lower, deserve a special mention: Upper for its medieval pulpit and seventeenth century helmet, and Lower for its unique atmosphere and almost unrestored appearance, complete with a west gallery, like Dunton.

Whitchurch could hardly be regarded as typically a Vale church, but it is well worth seeing on account of its fine proportions, tower, arcades and remains of wall painting. At nearby Hardwick is a most touching memorial in the churchyard. It is only Victorian in date, but records the burial of a number of bodies found during works at Holman's Bridge just outside Aylesbury, reckoned to be the victims of a Civil War skirmish. It records that here, buried in a common grave, rest friend and foe alike, and expresses the pious hope that never again may Englishman lift hand against Englishman. A sentiment we can all echo, though this does not inhibit us from taking up arms in defence of the architectural, historical and cultural heritage we all value so greatly.

E. CLIVE ROUSE
1972

Comfrey grows by the path leading down to Lower Winchendon Church. Comfrey fritters are among the less eccentric of 'wild' foods; the leaves can be stripped off, dipped into cold water, then in batter, and thence into a sizzling frying pan. They emerge like green-and-gold fish.

SUSAN COWDY
1971

'We always called this the workhouse. Each cottage had one so that the lace could be kept there out of the stir and dust.'

As she spoke, the old lacemaker emerged into her sitting-room-cum-kitchen from a closet with a good window but scarcely worthy of being called a room.

I had recently acquired an old thatched cottage myself in the district and it had just such a chamber which I had combined with another to make a bigger living room. For weeks I had been wondering what possible function such a small space could have served.

'When I was six,' she went on, 'my aunt first set me down on a stool with a 'pillow' and taught me how to use the bobbins. Soon I had to produce so many inches of lace each day before I could go out to play.'

The little old lady had a sad, interesting story to tell. When she and her sister were mere babies, her father had gone off to America. Soon after, her mother died. The children went to an aunt who lived in a whitewashed cottage nestling between church and manor.

Perhaps the father died, at any rate he was never heard of again. The aunt had a hard life housing, feeding and clothing herself and the two little nieces. She was up betimes in the morning setting the home in order because every possible moment must be spent at the pillow. And the children had to learn lacemaking as soon as their tiny fingers could hold the bobbins.

In summer and autumn there were added tasks. The hedgerows must be searched for wild fruits. Not only the lace and eggs, but heavy baskets of raspberries, blackberries, sloes, crabapples and damsons, had to be carried three miles along the hot, dusty road to Buckingham market. Then came the 'leasing' at harvest-time when it was a major disaster if they failed to glean enough for their year's supply of bread. After thrashing in their own small barn, the grain was taken to the mill down by the Ouse to be ground. The mill still stands there and serves the local farmers. Afterwards the flour was dragged home in sacks to be carefully stored away.

Their meals were frugal in the extreme, often only a sup of tea and a piece of rather unpalatable home-made bread. The cottage ovens were primitive and the baking seldom rose. A piece of white 'baker's-bread' was a great treat. So were eggs for they must be sold at market.

Youth in those days had a short childhood and scarcely any schooling. Miss Palmer went when she was eleven as maid-of-all-work to the vicarage and was counted very lucky to find such a good 'place'. It was, and still is, a rambling old building, and there were twelve children and a carriage and pair! But the little maid was happy with this large family and loved playing with the children. After all she was but a child herself and probably this was the most carefree time of her life.

Later she went into service in London. Never robust, bad health eventually forced her to retire to her native village when in her early fifties. She took up lacemaking again, and by a stroke of good luck she was able to settle in the fairy-tale cottage in which I found her.

I often made my way there. In spite of her under-privileged youth she was extremely well-informed and widely-read. She had a fine mind and brain. As we chatted the bobbins flew to and fro in her delicate nimble fingers and the lace grew as if by magic. While she worked she told me all sorts of traditions and stories connected with the industry.

The pillow she used was a tightly stuffed straw bolster which had belonged to her grandmother. It must have been well over a hundred years old even then. Some of the bobbins were quite plain, of bone or wood. Others were elaborately carved or had insets of brass or silver. A few even had phrases or names pricked out on them in red or black, and all had clusters of coloured beads or charms at the end to weigh them on the pillows. Those were called 'spangles'. It had been the custom for the village lads to carve and whittle the bobbins as offerings to their sweethearts and womenfolk at such anniversaries as Christmas and birthdays.

Bone was used for the first bobbins, from birds, rabbits and sheep; hence the name 'Bone-lace'. They were often greatly treasured and handed down from generation to generation. It is related that one was given by a girl to her sweetheart who carried it with him as a sort of talisman all through the

Crimean War. On it was pricked 'Forsake me not my Love'. He returned safely to restore it to her and soon after they were happily married.

Pins also played an important rôle in lacemaking. The earliest were fashioned from fish and bird bones cut in the shape of thorns. Those for holding the bobbins out of the way when not in use had heads of red sealing-wax. Others were used to mark the pattern pricked on the paper which was bound round the pillow. The pins were moved as the lace grew. Later brass pins were used because they did not rust. But for long they were too expensive.

Thread too was not cheap; it was made of flax. At one period when this was scarce silk thread was used and black silk lace became quite a vogue.

In the dark winter days and nights a round bowl of water was placed between the pillow and a homemade rush light to cast a soft glow on the work. They were called flashes and enabled several lacemakers to work from one source of light. Candles were luxuries and the rushes were peeled and coated with mutton-fat which was plentiful.

Lacemaking in England seems to have existed in a primitive form since the fourteenth century. Finer laces became fashionable in Elizabethan times, and the industry had fresh blood injected into it around 1570 when the Flemish lacemakers revolted against almost feudal oppression. They fled to England and settled at Olney, Newport Pagnell and neighbouring villages.

Traditionally the work was introduced to Buckinghamshire by Catherine of Aragon who is said to have excelled at it and at embroidery as well. She owned several manors in the county, and Henry VIII gave her Claydon. A lace called 'Catherine of Aragon's Lace' was still being produced around Towcester at the beginning of this century. It was coarser than Buckinghamshire pillow-lace and distinctly Spanish in character. The Queen's ladies are said to have taught it to the villagers.

Lace often figures in the dress accounts of Queen Elizabeth I, while Henrietta Maria, wife of Charles I, thought so highly of Buckinghamshire lace that she sent a present of it to the Queen of France. Even the taciturn William III seems to have had a weakness for it. In 1695 there is an entry of 117 yards for trimming pocket handkerchiefs, 78 yards for cravats, and two hundred and seventy pounds-worth for embellishing razor-cloths! The total comes to £2,459 19s. His wife, Queen Mary, was less extravagant: her expenditure for the previous year came to a mere £1,918!

In the reign of George III, Buckinghamshire lace became extremely popular. A particularly fine variety was made in Aylesbury. It was so much admired in Paris that it was copied there and sold as *'dentille d'Angleterre'*.

So from the early seventeenth century the Buckingham workers enjoyed comparative prosperity. From then on Buckinghamshire and Devonshire were looked upon as the great centres of the lacemaking industry in this country. In 1626 a school was founded at Great Marlow to teach boys and girls to knit, spin and make lace, and others followed, sometimes in cottages.

From Buckinghamshire the industry spread to Bedfordshire, Northants and Oxfordshire.

In and around Hanslope there was more lace made than anywhere else in the shire. Out of a population of 1,275 in 1801, 800 were engaged in the work. Many of them were children of both sexes who followed the occupation all their lives. The lace was sold at from sixpence to two guineas the yard, depending upon quality and width. In the sixteenth century it had been sold by weight!

Women preferred lacemaking to working in the fields. It was more profitable and they could take it up in any spare moment. Even busy married women often earned a pound a week by it. At the time a labourer's wage was about ten shillings a week, so this was a handsome addition to a family's finances.

St Andrew is the patron saint of lacemaking and till towards the end of the nineteenth century, 30th November was kept as a holiday. It was called 'Tandering Feast', no doubt a corruption of Andrew. In some districts the name was 'Catterns Day' after Catherine of Aragon.

Eventually Maltese and Torchon laces were brought over to England and people found it easier and quicker to copy those coarser varieties.

The Buckinghamshire lace trade was destroyed by the introduction of cheap machine-made Nottingham lace in the late nineteenth century. This has long been out of fashion. However, I recently read that it is again being sought after, owing to the present craze for 'Victoriana'! No accounting for tastes!

But there are still, and will probably always be, those who possess and treasure hand-made lace. Only a few weeks ago at a performance at Covent Garden I noticed a slender, elegant elderly woman with beautifully dressed silvery hair. She wore a perfectly cut gown of midnight-blue and its sole adornment was a delicate collar of exquisite Buckinghamshire pillow-point.

ANNE CRAIG HOWIE
'Lacemaking in Buckinghamshire',
Bucks Life, March 1967

Disraeli was always particularly anxious for the welfare of the agricultural labourer, and I do not forget how, in one of his speeches at the meeting of the Bucks Agricultural Association, in speaking of the sanitary condition and the better housing of labourers, he said, 'In building cottages there are three absolutely necessary things to be provided – an oven, a tank, and a porch.' This is practical advice; and in his Manchester speech I find the following, which perhaps may shock the sensitive nerves of many of my agricultural friends. 'And in the first place,' he said, 'to prevent any misconception, I beg to express my opinion that an agricultural labourer has as much right to combine for the bettering of his conditions as a manufacturing labourer or a worker in metals.' Again, he said, 'Gentlemen, I should deeply regret to see the tillage of this country reduced and a recurrence to pasture take place. I should regret it principally on account of the labourers themselves. Their new friends call them 'Hodge', and describe them as a feeble body, and stolid in mind. That is not my experience of them – I believe them to be a stalwart race, sufficiently shrewd and open to reason. I would say to them with confidence, as the great Athenian said to the Spartan who rudely assailed him, 'Strike, but hear me!'

J. F. K. FOWLER
Echoes of Old County Life, 1892

The village has never been quite the same since the cottagers stopped breeding ducks for the London market. Once they were so much a part of our life that we could not have imagined the ponds and greens without them. The ponds now look forsaken, as though themselves admitting that they have ceased to serve their true purpose. Their waters once so clear are turbid and overgrown with weeds, and the beautiful pool in front of the church goes dry in the summer, as if in despair, as it rarely did when ducks sported there.

Except when snow covered the ground, and the water froze, so that they could not wash themselves, our ducks' large pure white bodies were a pleasant sight. Whether on the ponds, tail up and head down, seeking some morsel in the mud at the bottom; or with flapping wings, chasing each other across the surface in a gambol of ecstasy; or sailing about in a mass formation, each with neck erect and head forwards; their movements were always graceful. Or, when in some wayside ditch they foraged, or on an April morning caught the large worms that lay half-way out of the earth on the village greens, their lives seemed to be ever infused with the proper village spirit – a rollicky, happy-go-lucky, carefree sort of existence, free from any concern for the morrow, and happy in the provision of the moment.

Their gait on land was perfectly matched to the even tenor of the village life. Each morning they walked its ways in line – the father drake, with his six to eight wives. He always led the way; they followed on behind; his eyes were always casting to right and left to know if the way was free from danger. It was delightful to watch, that waddling line of white passing over the carpet of deep green, every neck and body zigzagging with every step. The sway sideways was caused by the weight of the bodies, which were large and had deep keels between short legs. One look showed how out of poise the body must be when momentarily supported by one leg or the other in the act of walking. It could only be done at all by alternately throwing the whole weight over from side to side. The drake and his retinue of ducks were selections from the batch of the previous year, and were called a clutch. They were chosen and retained for breeding; or, to be more exact, they produced the eggs, which were always hatched by hens. In the laying season every duck faithfully laid one egg every day. The owner kept them all imprisoned until this duty had been done. There, loudly quacking, with only a rude door between themselves and freedom, they impatiently demanded his arrival. He waited only to see the last egg laid; then he opened the door, and a mad scramble began, which quickly settled down into the proper, regular march in line, as, led by the drake, all headed together for their distant pond.

That was the daily march, so much a part of the life to which we all grew up that no one imagined it would ever cease to be. The ponds were the common meeting-places; the clutches of various owners met there and swam as one community for the day. The passion and glory of their life being swimmable water, they made what haste ducks could, always pausing at each chance puddle on the way to dip each bill once as they went by. But should danger of dog or other fearsome form be seen, then the march in line changed to a medley of disorder till the worst was passed, when each tail would wag at once in confident assurance; and the march would be resumed. As soon as the pond came into view, their gait quickened; the waddle became a run for the margin, where all lined up and drank to the day ahead, each filling its broad bill and raising its head to feel water's cool flow down the throat.

They assembled clutch by clutch, the firstcomers ever ready to welcome those that followed. The drakes knew no jealousy. When they saw another clutch approaching, they swam to the margin to welcome them. The pond was their citadel of safety, a domain of their own, free from the intrusion of man or beast. On sunny days and dreary alike, their quackings still sounded like a note of joy. There, while the hours tolled by, and children's voices from the school made melody in hymn and song, everybody's ducks swam together, or gambolled to and fro, or dived, or lay at ease on the broad-spreading grass.

So the day passed – its hours told off by the old bell within the grey church tower; and martins wheeled around in flight all day, or swerving, skimmed the water's surface for the fly, or sought its brink for mud for building nests. Those hours seemed much the same except for the changing numbers counted out by the deep-toned bell. Yet the ducks knew their time, whether by bell or by some inward sense, and at their hour they left the pond and formed again in clutch.

Then eastward, westward, northward, long swaying lines of white were seen, each line a drake with his ducks behind him treading through the deep-grown grass. All their diverging pathways led from pond to home, a rough shed with corn and straw within for food and rest.

At the cottage homesteads to which they all were going, a very different order of duck life was going forward. There ducklings of all ages of up to eight or ten weeks were to be seen, penned in shallow enclosures on the garden ground. The pens were made of thin boards about eighteen inches

Haddenham Church and duckpond.

high, fixed edgewise by stakes. The cottagers came to our yard to buy them. When making the pens, you had to be very careful not to leave any crevice through which a duckling could pass its head and commit accidental suicide. They lived a precarious, delicate life that demanded incessant watchfulness. Intense sunshine on their heads would turn them giddy; so there had to be some protective awning or board under which they could creep. An unexpected shower that wetted their feathers was dangerous in another way; for warmth afterwards they were inclined to huddle together and thus contract chills; so they were kept on the move after a shower until the feathers had dried.

    A stock duck seldom showed any desire to hatch her own eggs. Indeed, it seemed to be in keeping with their carefree dispositions that hens should do it for them. Sitting hens, for sale or hire, were in great demand throughout the season; heavy cross-breeds, with some feather on the legs were preferred. The orange box, with its three compartments, was largely used for setting;

one hen on thirteen duck eggs to each part. The boxes were placed end to end in rows on the floor of a shed specially designed for that purpose. Silence reigned; scores of hens in semi-darkness sat out their four weeks of parental durance.

The task was really nothing but an imposition; for after faithfully sitting and hatching the young ducks, the hen was rarely allowed to have them for more than a day or so. She was turned adrift in the run instead, and the ducklings were kept in a shallow box and fed with hard-boiled egg chopped up with boiled rice, to which a little fine meal was added. It was imperative that a saucer of water should be at hand for them to wet their bills in. Throughout the eight or ten weeks of their lives feeding was graded according to their advance in size. When they were large enough, scalded greaves, the residue of the tallow-chamber – mixed with pollard and later on barley meal – became the staple food with which they gorged themselves and rapidly put on delicate flesh. Enclosed in the pens they had little exercise, and their proneness to eating soon made them lazy with weight. The body became too large for the strength of the legs. Filled with good food, they drowsed away the greater part of the few weeks that constituted their lives; to them an experience of ease, sunshine and plenty.

When they were about half-grown, they were driven to a pond to have their one and only swim, which helped them to feather properly. It was not unusual to meet a flock that covered the whole road from side to side, each a little ball of yellow fluff, merrily chirping as it walked. There were no motor-cars in those days, and the horse-drawn vehicle simply had to stop until they had passed. Unlike chickens, they were easily controlled; their disposition was to keep together in a flock, and they always appeared to be enjoying themselves. The owners had their special call, 'Dill! Dill! Dill!' for ducklings, in imitation of the sounds that they made. The call was not used when they grew older.

It was a treat to see them all take the water; to watch them head off bravely over its surface, then dive and flap their little wings in natural delight. That was one of the few pleasures of duck breeding, but those who had the responsibility in hand declared that all the rest was incessant work and worry. 'Duckling' – as the industry was called – was 'nothing but moil and groil, work from light to dark, for as long as the season lasted.'

And this was true: it was no light matter to be responsible for some hundreds of young lives; to attend to their parents – the sitting hens – daily; to cook their food as they grew older; to clean and prepare the pens and guard against emergencies, housing them safely each night on clean straw. At the same time, there were the fully grown to be killed and plucked ready for market. This was done in the early morning, and after plucking they were placed in a cold chamber to cool off before being packed for transit by rail. Many labourers' wives, I knew, did all this alone, except for an occasional help of women at the plucking, for which they were paid three-halfpence a duck. Their husbands were away at regular work on a farm, and could only give a hand in the evening. The money that duckling brought was hardly earned, for often the price dropped as low as half a crown per head. Yet some folk saved enough by it to buy their own cottages; and now and then the thriftiest made it their first stepping stone to rise above the position of a labourer, and eventually to take land on their own as small farmers.

The ducks for market were collected late each afternoon. A large cob, drawing a covered cart, which had a trundling sound that we all recognised as the duckman, went round the district, delivering empty hampers called 'flats', and collecting others filled with dead ducks. The duckman acted as agent for the Smithfield salesmen and issued their consignment notes to the breeders, one of which, stating the number of ducks and name of the owner, was placed in each hamper. He paid over the money on a subsequent call, handing to each breeder a salesman's voucher of the price made, from which his own agent's fee was deducted. The demand was at its best when green peas were in season; and so the aim of each breeder was to catch the early market.

A cottage garden given over to duck breeding was not an inviting sight, and the stench after a warm June shower was even worse to put up with. Hard work, worry, and bad smell; no wonder the village held duckling mildly in disrepute; so that the dwellers in what was properly called Duck Lane changed the name to Flint Street instead. A local sickness called 'duck fever' was formerly prevalent; it was said to come from the smell of the ducklings. No matter what efforts were made to keep them clean, the paddling feet of young ducks, and their continual need of water caused the pens to be always dirty with slime. And one villager would say to another over the duck-pens: 'I wonder what those who'll eat them would say if they could see the places where they are bred.'

WALTER ROSE
Good Neighbours, 1942

A typical Ferdy whim produced one of the greatest sights of Southern England. In 1874, magic began to transpire at Lodge Hill, as desolate and deserted a spot as could be found in Buckinghamshire. Ferdy had bought it and 2,700 acres of environs from the Duke of Marlborough, for some £200,000. Ferdy happened to like the view. To make this vantage point habitable, the entire top of the hill was sliced off. Water must be hauled from fourteen miles away. A special steam tramway with a track fourteen miles long had to be built to transport materials from the nearest rail station. Numerous driveways with a manageable gradient were hewn into the slopes. Teams of Percheron mares, imported for the purpose from Normandy, toiled up the rise with building stuff.

Waddesdon Manor, built by Baron Ferdinand de Rothschild in the latter part of the nineteenth century, stands in over two thousand acres of plantation and park land overlooking the village of Waddesdon. Designed in the French Renaissance style, the Manor houses a priceless collection of pictures and furnishings which represent some of the finest work of the seventeenth and eighteenth centuries. Bequeathed to the National Trust in 1957 by Mr James de Rothschild, Waddesdon is one of the country's most treasured properties.

A wilderness was coerced into a park through topographical surgery, drainage, irrigation, and the wholesale planting of shrubberies. Acres of flowerbeds were sown. Since Ferdinand placed his woods as conveniently as other people place their ashtrays, he had hundreds of trees transplanted. Since he liked large chestnuts, sixteen horses were needed to move each one; the telegraph wires by the roadside must be lowered for their passage. The whole thing was rounded out with the customary terraces, aviaries, rookeries, fountains, and groups of seventeenth-century statuary by Girardon, an important Versailles sculptor.

What house could fit such an estate? Ferdy decreed a select anthology of his favourite French castles. Into his mansion of mansions he incorporated the two towers of the Château de Maintenon, the dormer windows of Anet, the chimneys of Chambord, two versions of the staircase of Blois (slightly smaller and glazed to fight off the English climate) – all 'suitably combined, edited and improved', one expert thought.

As to interior décor, Ferdinand sometimes had the panelling specially carved to accommodate outsize paintings like Guardi's two vast views of Venice. More usually he contented himself with ready-made wares – that is, with the finest boiseries (decorative panelling), extracted from the most luxurious Louis XV and Louis XVI Hotels in Paris, brought across the Channel and integrated artfully into the various apartments. The furniture consisted largely of peacock pieces made for the Royal Family in France. The carpeting constituted the world's largest collection of Savonneries, so named after the workshop of their origin, whose products went exclusively to the Bourbons. The ceilings, Beauvais tapestries, Sèvres porcelain and *objets* (including a big musical elephant) matched the foregoing and each other. Canvases by Reynolds, Gainsborough, Cuyup, Pater, Van der Heyden – not to speak of those by Watteau and Rubens later added by heirs – were almost legion.

After more than a decade of creation there rose above the English countryside an immense French Renaissance mirage, glistening in white marble, resplendent with 222 rooms. Ferdy rested and thought it good. He called it Waddesdon Manor. To this day it remains an absolutely stunning circumvention of cosiness.

All the world came to see and gasp. At his Saturday to Monday parties (the weekend was practised but not yet named in the *fin de siècle*) the host would entertain the Shah of Persia, the German Emperor, Henry James, Robert Browning, Guy de Maupassant. (The Aga Khan and a series of Prime Ministers from Balfour to Winston Churchill are also found in the guest book). Bertie honoured one of the Blois staircases by breaking a royal ankle on it.

Rumours of the phenomenon reached Victoria's ear. On May 14, 1890, Her Majesty did a nearly unprecedented thing. She called on a private individual. She had to see for herself what this Rothschild had wrought out of a bare hill.

FREDERIC MORTON
The Rothschilds, 1962

If you read old books, you will constantly meet references to 'country quiet' and to green nature as a refuge from 'the chargeable noise of the great town'. Was it once so? A sixth-century Collect begins: 'Be present, O merciful God, to protect us through the SILENT hours of the night.' This was written in the 'Dark Ages'; a darker one might regard it as a copyist's error for 'strident', and for modern silence day or night one goes to town. Silence is one of the lost arts, like solitude, and Milton's 'Silence was pleased' at the nightingale's song is to us altogether a dream. It is hard for us to hear any bird's song, and indeed to hear out-of-doors one's own or a fellow-being's voice. The Devil's two greatest enemies are music and silence. When quiet comes, it is a hush rather than a silence, a brief suspension and breathing pause before the accustomed harsh uproar. The whole outside nature is so jangled and out of tune that normality of any kind is 'a sweet surprise'. How blessed are the fogs and mists that bring us silence indeed! One sips the quietude like some choice and rare vintage; one listens to the silence as to Bach's 'Sheep may safely graze'. It is our 'balm of hurt minds', a healing power, a gentle dew, a green thought in a green shade, a knitting up of the ravell'd sleeve of care, a benediction like rest after violent exertion, medicinal, restorative.

> Eternal silence, sing to me,
> And beat upon my whorled ear,
> Pipe me to pastures still and be
> The music that I care to hear.

For an analogy to the aeroplane it is necessary to think back into the Jurassic Period when the pterodactyls oared themselves above the steaming swamps. One August day when I sat under the vine, I had the flash of a closer similitude. Is it air which these monsters navigate? No, it is water. This earth is the bed of the deep sea and great devil-fish prowl to and fro above it with rigid fins, blunt snouts and leaden bodies, while high above THEM is the surface of the ocean, broken into dark waves and combing breakers and lit by gleams of the sun above both water and ocean floor. The tractors crawling over the surface of our undersea world look like squids or enormous crabs, while the huge scrapers that tear the corn off the ground and the topsoil with it to make an aerodrome, are other forms of crustaceans that people our depths. We are deep in the glooms of the abyssal waters, long before Amphioxus got him a four-chambered heart and lungs that the air caressed and sunbeams filled. Our lives too are those of the deep sea creatures; we crawl anxiously about and, when danger threatens from the predators above us, we burrow in the mud like fearful flat-fish. We move in scared shoals and everywhere above our subaqueous depths the armoured ganoids and primeval sharks which rule the abysses prey upon themselves and us.

These marvellous engines of destruction are very brave and brilliant; they perform incredible feats; if some prey on us, others save us. But this whole opaque world in which we live is a world of deepest night, and to find light we must RETURN TO EARTH and what is above and beyond the earth.

I look once more down the garden and try to project myself into it, as Keats projected himself into the sparrow pecking on the gravel. The garden, the fields, the parish that George Russell called 'the cradle of the nation', how can we grope our way back to them? Not back into the past since they are only incidentally of the past. They are the permanent conditions of life set out by eternity for our span of temporality. Perhaps we can only readjust ourselves to them by the necessity of chaos, that is to say, through a fearful experience that the giant affront to these conditions is failure. For we must grow things or die, and though we are temporarily doing so, the whole weight of urban civilisation is against the garden, the fields and the parish. Not the least factor in the disintegration of rural life is the aerodrome which sucks up the village population and drowns its way of life, with hardly less effect than its injury to the soil. Almost as disruptive is the scandal of the casual labourer or the daughter of a land-labourer making more at the aerodrome than he, one of the last survivors of the skilled worker, can make on the land. As an old country-woman of eighty-eight said with that profound and unconscious poetry once 'in widest commonality spread', these aerodromes and other works like them are 'distressing' to the land.

H. J. MASSINGHAM
'Nostalgia For Silence',
This Plot of Earth, 1944

> March will search
> and April will try
> And May will tell if you live or die.
> > (The blacksmith at Terrick gave this rhyme
> > to the Rev. C. White of Ellesborough)

I am the last person alive who knew Florence Nightingale well and loved her dearly and remember her vividly. In addition I have many hundreds of letters written in her own beautiful handwriting and kept chronologically in eight boxes as well as seven boxes of letters about her. It is sad to have to relate that she and her sister never got on well together. Parthenope – Parthe to everyone except me – born in 1819, thought how lucky Florence was to have such a charming elder sister, a view not held by Florence. When Florence was ten the sisters were apart and Florence writes to Parthe, 'Pray let us love one another better than we have done; it is the will of God, and Mama especially desires it.' But even Mama with the help of the Almighty could not achieve that. It was nobody's fault. Parthe was not merely a competent artist but a really good one, and lived for a social life; Florence was better looking and much cleverer and always anxious to help others, with no use for social life.

Another problem was education. There was of course no school for girls born about 1820. Lord Melbourne seems to have typified the normal attitude: 'I would rather have men about me when I am ill; I think it requires very strong health to put up with women.' Also he is reputed to be the author of the saying, 'Generally speaking, women are generally speaking.' Fortunately Mr Nightingale was a brilliant teacher and under his tuition the girls spoke fluent French, German and Italian; however, when it came to mathematics, statistics, Latin and Greek, Parthe said, 'No thank you,' but Florence lapped it up and became a fine scholar ready later to discuss abstruse points of Greek with Benjamin Jowett, Master of Balliol. Mrs

Nightingale died just before I was born, so I never saw her; but my Mother told me she was very beautiful and found in Parthe the exact daughter she wanted; she never understood Florence.

Of the Crimean War itself, all my letters and information have been incorporated in Mrs Woodham Smith's quite excellent biography. The soldiers soon found an anagram for FLORENCE NIGHTINGALE: FLIT ON CHEERING ANGEL. The fact needs emphasising that miraculous as was the work she did during the Crimean War, her service to the world was even greater from the end of that war until the end of the century when her powers began to flag. On returning home with hardly anybody knowing even by sight this young lady of thirty-six — there were no photographs — she devoted herself primarily to work for the Army. She proved that more deaths were due in the Crimea to preventable disease than to the War; and then a year later she published figures proving that mortality in barracks was double the mortality in civil life.

Then gradually she concentrated on hospitals and nurses. It would not be an exaggeration to say that all hospitals built during the last hundred years owe something to the essentials she put forward. The Royal Bucks Hospital at Aylesbury was dominated by her personality; the King of Portugal asked her to design a hospital in Lisbon. She never seemed to be wrong. Men dislike a woman who is never wrong. But this accuracy was ensured because her brother-in-law Sir Harry Verney, M.P., was constantly asking questions of ministers in the House of Commons, on Florence's behalf. Instead of being known as M.P. for Buckingham, he became Member for Miss Nightingale. So with nurses, Florence Nightingale dreamt of girls giving up all to serve the sick; she lived to see her dream come true.

One of the most remarkable tributes was paid her by Doctor Sutherland. He gave up his life to working with and for her. He writes: 'Nobody who has not worked with her daily could have an idea of her strength of mind, her extraordinary powers joined with her brilliant intellect. She was one of the most gifted creatures God ever made.'

When the Indian Mutiny broke out she studied the Indian problems and soon became *the* expert on sanitation and irrigation. It seems to be true that almost every Viceroy between the end of the Mutiny and the end of the century consulted her before going out. The last was Lord Elgin (1895); when I became his son-in-law he told me how much he had learnt from her though she had never been in India.

An unexpected illustration of her administrative genius came to light recently. In 1947, the Government appointed a select Committee on estimates, 'To enquire into the methods adopted by Accounts in all Departments of State.' The Committee reported that in only one department was administration on really sound lines, and that was in the Medical Department of the War Office. So the officer in charge was sent the file and it was found that the system had been inaugurated by Florence Nightingale in 1859, eighty-eight

Claydon, which has been the home of the Verney family since 1620, cannot accurately be dated, but it is presumed to have been built long before it was first occupied by the Verneys. It was much altered in the eighteenth century by Ralph, the second Earl Verney; the large stable court was also added at this period. The interior decoration of the house, with its ornamental plasterwork and wood carving, is exceptionally rewarding, and the superb staircase considered one of the most beautiful in England. Florence Nightingale, whose sister, Parthenope, married Sir Harry Verney, 2nd Baronet, spent much of her time at Claydon; her bedroom and a museum devoted mainly to her work are on the first floor.

years previously.

Now for the personal memories. There is a letter from Florence to her brother-in-law, dated 10th June 1881 saying, 'I am glad Margaret is safe and thank God she has a boy.' I am the boy born 7th June 1881, at Rhianva. I claim to have begun to take notice in the year of Queen Victoria's Jubilee when I was six and a constant visitor to Claydon, my first visit being to be christened by Dean Fremantle who came back to his old parish for that purpose. Florence Nightingale was in her sixties, and by then used to come to Claydon often for months at a time. Her two homes, Embley and Lea Hurst, had been left entailed on a male by Mr Nightingale, and so Claydon was the obvious solution. My memory tells me that I used to see her daily till I was sent to school as unmanageable. I used to get constant messages from the Blue Room, Florence Nightingale's sitting room. On my part I prepared questions; she always knew the answers. What bird did this feather come from? What was the correct name of the lovely wild rose? On her (part), a wren 'about the size of a walnut' came to her bird table and needed a fresh bone; off I went to the kitchen, bringing back and fixing a new bone. She always seemed to take my side, which a small boy appreciated; so if in trouble one would go to her for comfort. I clearly remember one incident. Was I eight? I was caught lying. So I rushed up to her, sobbing. What was I to do? 'Tell me all about it.' 'I broke something and said John had broken it.' 'We have all lied in our time. Go downstairs and tell your parents that when they were your age *they* lied.' How comforting; of course I never did, but if *they* lied it could not be so very wicked. . . .

To make this slight record true, I ought to add that the gulf between the two sisters widened. Though so constantly the guest of her sister, the two never met. Indeed there is a distressing letter that she will see anyone except Parthe.

Of course it is preposterous to pretend that as a small boy I realised the greatness of Florence Nightingale, but as I grew up I think I can truthfully claim that through my prep school and Harrow days I did begin to understand that, before her mind gave way, my beloved great aunt, perfect as an aunt, was more than that, and by the time I went up to her beloved Balliol in 1900, I doubt if she knew who I was; I do not think she came to Claydon in this century though she lived till 1910. She died in London and was buried in West Wellow Cemetery. All the great attended a vast memorial service in St Paul's Cathedral, while a small party – I was one of them – laid her to rest near her old home of Embley.

Since then during the last seventy years I have realised to the full what her life has meant to the world. During the many months she spent in her old age at Claydon House she rather took Steeple Claydon under her wing, assisting many with advice and financial help. The village was slow to adopt the Public Libraries Act and to have a flourishing library. She saw that it must come in spite of a reactionary parish council, and she gave a cheque for £50 to be cashed in the future. That cheque is now in the Parish Hall. But still there is no memorial in this countryside. . . .

Two quotations must end my tribute. First a Diary she gave me in 1895 and inscribed in her handwriting.

'For our dear Harry with Aunt Florence's love; and may each day of this New Year 1895 be better and happier than yesterday, and may the young boy and the old woman make and find this a better and happier year than any that has gone before. So help us God. – New Year's Day, 1895.'

Last, a personal letter from Doctor Jowett, Master of Balliol, to Florence Nightingale, dated 1879.

'Nobody knows how many lives are saved by your Nurses, how many thousand soldiers are now alive owing to your forethought and diligence, how many natives of India (they might be counted probably by hundreds of thousands) have been preserved by the energy of a sick lady who can scarcely rise from her bed, but *I* know it. Signed, Benjamin Jowett.'

And I, Harry Verney, know it too.

SIR HARRY VERNEY
'Florence Nightingale, 1820–1910'
Bucks Life, February 1970

An old Bucks man sang:
>Here we suffer grief and pain
>Near the hills they do the same,
>So they do next-door.

What we romantically call 'Danewort', from a rather late belief that its autumn-bloody, autumn-tattered colonies grow where Danes fell in battle, has been known for some two thousand years, at the very least as a strong purgative. It grows by roads, in obstinate, isolated colonies. It does not spread much in normal vegetation, and seems to need ground where the competition is not severe or consistent. It is a plant which may have come north about 12,000–9,000 B.C., as the glaciers of the Ice Age diminished and the vegetation increased. This Danewort (or Dwarf Elder) would have begun a struggle for existence until at last it could maintain itself where man unwittingly gave it help, along road verges, etc. The colony alongside the road at Cuddington, for example, grows in a deep ditch which is not cut by tidy-minded local roadmen.

GEOFFREY GRIGSON
A Herbal of All Sorts, 1959

Towards evening of a calm, lovely day I reached the little North Buckinghamshire village where I was to live for the next twenty years. The ancient moated house on its outskirts which was to be my home was still in the hands of the builders and decorators. I can even now recall the faces of the local worthies who were the unchanging members and employees of the firm that carried out the work and who, during the next three intensely exciting, yet peaceful weeks, were to become my allies and friends.

Until the house was ready for occupation I had arranged to stay in the village post-office half-a-mile away – 'a cottage well thatched with straw' – kept by some of the kindest people I have ever met. Thence every morning

Spring scene at Monks Risborough.

my wife and I set out along a grassy, out-grown, elm-bordered lane which took us, without crossing or touching a road, to the old white house, with its tall Elizabethan chimneys and beautiful red-brick seventeenth century wall, on which all our immediate worldly hopes and interests had become centred. Beside us walked a great, thick-ruffed, deep-chested dog, of Gladstonian dignity, wolf-like appearance and almost unbelievable gentleness, who from the first moment adopted his future home as though he had always lived there and already knew that beneath the grass of its quiet lawn, sheltered from wind and sound by high yew hedges, he was to find after seven happy years his eternal resting-place. Then, until we returned for our evening meal down the elm-lined lane, each calm September day passed in a whirl of activity as we supervised and helped – or hindered – builder and gardener, unpacked boxes of books, papers, china and glass, arranged the furniture and hung the pictures as each room was made ready for habitation. I can still see the glittering white of the newly-distempered walls and the beautiful brown oak of the beams stripped of their many coats, the shining elm staircase, the vast fireplace we undug in one room and the carved Jacobean overmantel of another, the ancient walnut and mahogany furniture we had brought with us which fitted into their places in their new home as though they had been made for it, and the seventeenth and eighteenth century ladies and gentlemen in their gilt frames who seemed to accept, so surprisingly and naturally, their new and humbler home as if it was part of the eternal order of things. They looked down as though they were happy, and as though the serenity of that enchanting, welcoming little house had won their hearts, as it had ours.

Outside were the gentle, rolling fields and guardian elms of the North Buckinghamshire plain, imperceptibly turning from green to gold as the warning of the first night frosts after those warm, sun-kissed misty days. There was no sound of anything but birds and human voices, of the cattle in the fields, and the distant noises of the quiet village street. All the houses in it were either of rosy seventeenth-century bricks, with high-pitched roofs, or of white-washed walls with half-timbering and thatch, and all stood almost hidden from one another and the world in groves and clusters of elms. There were no aeroplanes, no sounds of wireless, no lights but the soft glow of oil lamps, round which we sat at night reading in a profound country quiet. The restless modern world existed, but it was still far away, though we were only fifty miles from London. I have never known so peaceful a place, or so gently a happy one, and that September for me was like a kind of honeymoon between man and earth, dweller and home. I became naturalised, as it were, into the quiet land I had chosen and which was to be my background for so long. There was no sense of strangeness, none of unfamiliarity; it was as though I had been born there, and even the beloved Wiltshire haunts of my boyhood did not seem more home than this. Perhaps it held such magic for me because this unassuming countryside drew its atmosphere from an incredibly ancient woodland past; once part of the forest of Bernwood, it constituted a watershed between the Norfolk pinewoods, where I was born, and the south-western beechwoods where I was bred. I cannot explain it, but can only record the fact of my sudden and glad enslavement and the love and gratitude I still feel for that friendly land of elms, sloping meadows, oaks and leafy hamlets, and for the benediction of the kindly autumn month in which I was made free of it.

SIR ARTHUR BRYANT
The Lion and the Unicorn, 1969

The late Earl of Lonsdale kept a pack of harriers at the Harcourt Arms Hotel by the Tring Station on the London and North-Western Railway, about thirty miles from town. The hounds were drafted from Mr Drake's and the Old Berkeley foxhounds, and a few from Baron Rothschild's staghounds; and these, with some large-framed harriers, made a rare combination of speedy dogs, and afforded capital sport on the offdays of the stag and foxhound meets. After a time his lordship experienced a great scarcity of hares

The Whaddon Chase, near Whitchurch.

in the Vale, and he was advised to bring down from his Cumberland estates some wild foxes and try what he could do with them, on those days when no hare could be found. The 'bag foxes', though they afforded excellent sport, were considered Cockney game, beneath the dignity of the real fox-hunter, and great fun was made of their doings. But the Earl was not to be beat, and he determined to see what he could do by hunting and training these Cumberland animals. The Station Hotel was kept by a rare old sportsman, Mr Sam Brown, a twin-brother of John Brown who rode his horse Confidence in the first Aylesbury Steeplechase in 1835 (these men were born in or about 1794, and only joined the majority two or three years since, at ninety-two and ninety-four years of age, and they rode young horses up to three or four years of their decease). There was a large barn adjoining the hotel, and inside it were arranged rows of cages, which contained the foxes; and within the building fences and rails were put up, and their keeper, 'the man with the broom' was accustomed every morning to stir up 'Reynard', and exercise him backwards and forwards over these artificial fences. On certain days, the Earl and the field would go out and look for a hare, when a man would come up and say, 'My Lud, I seed a fox go away yonder.' 'Thank you, my man,' the Earl would reply, giving him half-a-crown; 'show me where.' Mr William Reid who lived at The Node, near Hitchin, and who hunted with the Hertfordshire, was so jealous of the sport these foxes gave that he composed some verses, which were inserted in *Bell's Life*, the then great sporting paper of the day; these were quoted and sung in almost every sporting county in England at that time.

THE CAPTIVE FOX

It was of an Earl with an ancient name,
Who hunted the fox, but preferr'd him tame,
Tho' his sire had been a keen hunter free
And bold as e'er rode o'er a grass countree.
That sire once mounted his well-bred horse,
And view'd the fox from the hillside gorse.
His son has come down by a second-class train,
Worried a bagman and home again.

'Tis half-past twelve by the station clocks,
And the Earl has call'd for his horse and fox.
Behind the good Earl there rides a groom,
And next comes a man with a big birch broom,
Wearing the Earl's discarded breeches,
Who will tickle the fox when he comes to the ditches.
The Earl's admirers are ranged in Brown's yard,
They all wear black boots, and mean to ride hard!
Either wily fox or the timid hare
Be the game today, none of them care;
It was well that the Earl had call'd for his fox,
And brought him from Tring in a little deal box.

Three hours or more they drew for a hare,
And drew all in vain, 'twas blank despair;
Then cried the Earl to the elder Brown,
'Open the box and turn him down.'
They turned him down in Aylesbury Vale,
In sight of a fence call'd post and rail,
To suit the views of a certain gent
Who rather liked rails and thought he 'went'.

Over the rails, the first to fly,
Was the jumping gent, but the fox was sly,
And would have declined, but the Earl and his groom,
The Huntsman and Whip, and the man with the broom,
And some boys in a cart, and the Browns, Sam and John,
Would not hear of his shrinking, and urged him on.

A pleasant line the captive took,
Avoiding the doubles and shirking the brook;
As you may imagine he went by rule,
Only taking the fences he learnt at school.

Five hounds of Baron Rothschild's breed,
Unmatch'd for courage and strength and speed,
Close on his flying traces they came,
And almost won the desperate game;
Just as the Earl prepared to sound
The dread 'Whoo Whoop', he went to ground;
So they dug him out, the Earl and his groom,
The Huntsman and Whip and the man with the broom.
The fox and the hounds are at Tring again,
And his lordship return'd by the four o'clock train.

J. F. K. FOWLER
Echoes of Old County Life, 1892

At the foot of Brill Hill, three-quarters of a mile north of the village, a few mounds in a field mark all that remains of the terminus of the Brill and Wotton Tramway, a piece of nineteenth-century ducal enterprise. On the other side of the road is Tramway Farm, and with the aid of the $2\frac{1}{2}$-inch ordnance survey map, other remains of the tracks, embankments and bridges can be found along the seven-mile course of the tramway between Brill and Quainton Road. Woodsiding Bridge, a short distance towards Wotton, is well preserved, and examples of the rolling stock and locomotives are in the Transport Museum, Clapham.

The tramway was the private property of the third and last Duke of Buckingham. He built it, starting in September 1870, to transport estate workers and livestock, and it cost him £1,250 a mile to build. After petitions,

Quainton Road Station and Railway Museum.

the Duke agreed to carry passengers, and in 1872, the track was extended for a further quarter of a mile from Wotton to Brill. The tramway company's offices were in Brill, and the general manager was R. A. Jones of the Duke's office staff. A timetable of 1887, shows that a speed of only four miles per hour was achieved, but this was due to the five intermediate stops and the fact that the guard had to open and shut an unspecified number of farm gates across the track!

In August 1905, the Metropolitan Railway took over local branch lines, including Quainton Road to Brill, and four trains a day were provided. This resulted in a heavy loss of nearly £4,000 a year. It was decided to close the line, and the last train (crowded with railway enthusiasts) ran on the 30th November 1935. An auction of fittings and equipment followed, and realised £72 7s. The station sign at Westcott fetched one shilling!

A further indication of the atmosphere of the tramway may be gathered from the 1873 Rulebook for the staff: 'Three prolonged screams from the whistle are to be sounded should assistance be needed in consequence of fire in the train . . . and also if the Driver should notice fire amongst crops on adjoining land.'

ROBERT GIBBS
Bucks Miscellany, 1891

In 1900, shopping was easy for anyone with a few shillings in his pocket, but as the average labourer's wage was from 12s to 17s a week, it did not leave much for the frills of life. We had no special delicacy made in the village, but all elderly people remember the delicious crumpets made by James Ray who lived down Frog Lane (quite different from the modern bought varieties), luscious and golden brown, at a half-penny each. He also made sugar buns at the same price, which he brought round in a flat basket covered with a white cloth, together with the most mouth-watering 'lardy cakes', sold hot from the oven, with their fragrance penetrating to the top of the lane. There were five bakers in the village, their output mostly cottage loaves, the detachable heads being so handy for the farm labourer's mid-day meal, along with a piece of fat bacon. There were innumerable small shops kept by widows and spinsters who sold everything. Their wares ranged from calico, boot laces, candles, aniseed balls, soap and peppermints to the more conventional line of groceries – on opening their doors one was nearly knocked down by the combination of aromas. The shop which is most remembered is the one kept in a thatched cottage in Town's End Square. Its owner was a Mrs Maria Cook who sold 'Cook's Lollies', large slabs of toffee, wrapped in squares of newspaper and selling at a farthing each. Her two granddaughters tell me the secret of her success was using the 'best butter'. She also sold antibilious pills at two a penny, and needles, tapes, pins, sugar, and cheese at twopence a quarter.

There was only one orthodox butcher in the village, but Charlie Markham, the pig killer, bought offal from the slaughter-house, boiling it in a huge cauldron in Braden's Yard. He also sold delicious saveloy sausages at a penny each – so large that they could be cut up to feed two small mouths. But it was for his pig killing that Charlie was famous and was in demand for miles around. At that time everyone kept a pig, usually 'one for sale and one for the house'. On the fateful day (for the pig) he appeared, performing the deed with great skill, coming back next day to singe the carcass and cut it up into suitable joints. Every part was used, the blood being made into hog or black puddings, the scraps from the head made into home-made brawn, with the ear cut up into thin strips. The trotters made jelly, but it was the chitterlings which were the favourite, especially a part called 'grandmother's night-cap'. This was fried up for tea, and favourite relatives would appear with jars, with hopes of a portion to take home.

There were many pedlars who wandered from house to house, the most remembered being 'Charlie six-a-foot', a little dwarf in a frock coat plus top hat, who would mend windows. There was an old man in a donkey cart who sold seeds – and another who sold paraffin and cheap kippers from Thame market. There were two Irishmen, who came once a year, walking with staves and packs on their backs – and a tall man from Thame, balancing a huge basket of crockery on his head. Elderly people tell me that it was their great joy to tease him with the hopes that he would drop the lot. These are just a few of the memories which I have been told by folk who have lived out their days in Long Crendon, and despite the hard times, look back with nostalgia to the past.

JOYCE DONALD
A Short History of Long Crendon, 1971

Apple Marmalade

6 lb. windfalls, or cooking apples, peeled, cored and cut up. ½ nutmeg; 4 lb. granulated sugar; 5 oz. root ginger (bruised and put in a bag); 4 cloves, or more, to taste; lemon juice (or essence) to taste. Cook apples in pan till slightly soft. Add all other ingredients and keep stirring till sugar is dissolved. Boil till stiff and slightly brown. Put into jam jars and tie down as for jam. Can be served with hot or cold cornflour, junket or cream.

Old Bucks Recipe

Cherry Brandy

1 lb. sugar
1 pint old ale
1 lb. Morello cherries
Put into earthenware crock. Stir once a day for three weeks. Stand one week and then strain and bottle.

Old Bucks Recipe

Milk Punch

To a gallon of Brandy put a gallon of new milk and a Gallon of Spring water two dozen of Lemons a pound of single refined sugar or more 4 or 5 nutmegs grated pare your Lemons very thin & steep the peel all night in the brandy sqees the lemons very well & mix alltogether in an earthen vessell then hang your flannell bag up & put it in to run keep putting it up till tis as fine as rock water put your milk to it boyling hot cover it close till tis cold then run it off.

JANE TYRINGHAM BERESFORD'S
Recipe Book
Nether Winchendon 1722-1727

Mutton Collops

Let a leg of mutton hang 4 or 5 days, then cut it in thin pieces the bignes of a crown, hack it with the back of a knife, put some butter in your saucepan. Make it prity hot but not brown, put some of your meat in keep it stiring till you see it hot thro'. Draw your gravy strong and brown, take 3 or 4 shalots, lemon peel, horse redish, a little Thyme, 3 or 4 anchoveys, mince all together very fine and put into your gravey to cook. Heat it over the fire put in your meat and a good piece of butter, keep it shaking all the while, a little red wine, and sqes in a lemon. Let your sauce be prity thick.

JANE TYRINGHAM BERESFORD'S
Recipe Book
Nether Winchendon, 1722–1727

Nether Winchendon is the home of the Spencer-Bernards, and has remained in the same family for over four hundred years. The first records of the house date back to 1162 when the property was granted to the monks of Notley Abbey. In 1571 it was sold to Thomas Tyringham, and thereafter passed by inheritance down to the present owner. Jane Tyringham Beresford, some of whose recipes are reproduced in this book, lived in the manor during the early eighteenth century; on her death the house was bequeathed to her first cousin, Sir Francis Bernard, who later became governor of the American colonies of New Jersey and Massachusetts. The Tyringham family motto: 'Bear and Forbear', appears on a shield on the southeast façade. Sir Scrope Bernard, son of Sir Francis, added the entrance towers and several rooms, which were completed in 1820.

Westphalia Hams
Rub every Ham over with four ounces of salt peter. The next day put bay salt, common salt and coarse sugar of each half a pound into a quart of stale strong beer adding a like quantity to every ham to be made at that time. Pour this boyling hot over your hams, let them ly a fort'nit in this pickle rubbing them over & turning them twice a day. Then smoke every ham over a fire of saw dust and fresh Horse litter from a stable for three days and three nights, the Horse litter must be fresh every night. After which smoke them over a wood fire like other bacon.

JANE TYRINGHAM BERESFORD'S
Recipe Book
Nether Winchenson, 1722–1727

Cough Mixture

Flax-seed	Ginger
Clove	Lemon
Sugar candy	Brown Sugar

Boil flax-seed with lemon rind and clove ginger for some time, then strain and add lemon juice, brown sugar and sugar candy. Boil again until all is dissolved. Dose: A teaspoon 3 or 4 times daily.

Old Bucks Recipe

Emulsion for cleaning dirty furniture
Linseed oil, 1 part
Vinegar, 1 part
Turpentine, 1 part
Methylated spirit, $\frac{1}{4}$ part
Mix together by shaking vigorously.

Old Bucks Recipe

Leather Dressing
Anhydrous Lanolin, 7 ounces
Beeswax, $\frac{1}{2}$ ounce
Cedarwood Oil, 1 fluid ounce
Hexane, 11 fluid ounces
Dissolve the beeswax in the Hexane first, then add the lanolin, lastly the cedarwood oil.

Old Bucks Recipe

When we were kids, the summers were long and hot and dry, and we pitched our tents in Farmer White's field by the river at Eythrope. Perhaps 'pitched our tents' is the wrong expression, for we really had no tents to pitch; but we made camp. Yes. That's what we did. We made camp.

And that was a really serious and complicated exercise. We had to cut the hazel poles and fashion the pegs and throw our sheets of canvas, sacking, ex-Army blankets and whatever else was available over the framework when it was built. That was our camp. When it was firmly pegged down we filled it several feet deep with long grass (or freshly-cut hay if we could manage to steal any) and we rolled on it until it flattened, and was soft and springy.

We built our fireplace with stones around a trench; we gathered firewood and we took turns to fetch the water. We swam and we went birdsnesting and we fished. We crawled out of bed and faced the cold morning air; we lit the fire and cooked bacon and eggs and smoky tea. We chased butterflies and moths. We snared a rabbit or two; we fished, and used set-lines for eels and perch, and when we caught them we cooked them. It was a point of honour with us that nature had to find some of our food. It was cheating if you brought too much with you.

I never knew anything that tasted better than fried eels or perch cooked in bacon fat, or potatoes baked in the embers of the fire at night.

We sat round that fire and whittled sticks and talked into the early hours of the morning, and finally crawled into our beds by the light of the old oil lantern.

That was how and where I learned to fish in the Vale of Aylesbury, and although fishing was but a part of the outdoor life we loved so much, it was an essential part of what is known as 'growing up'. It was sheer joy, uncomplicated by those problems known only to adults. We had seven whole weeks of it. And it never rained!

There were a hundred brooks and streams to fish; a thousand trees to climb. We served our apprenticeships with the smaller fish, and we learned that the so-called 'mud gudgeon' was a lover of clean gravel, and that it could not tolerate mud. We learned that the 'Whiskery Dick' was the stone loach, and that it, too, thrived in clean and unpolluted water. We dangled small worms on cotton lines devoid of hooks and caught 'bannies', 'bannistickles', and 'cock-firies', which were, of course, common sticklebacks. Then we graduated to the bigger fish with which our streams, ponds and lakes abounded.

Kindly keepers from the neighbouring estates of Hartwell and Eythrope turned a blind eye on our activities and allowed us to learn our craft. It was not until later years that we realised how privileged we had been in those early days. We gradually began to understand the need for stealth and concealment, or as Walton put it, to 'study to be quiet', and we progressed from being noisy, half-naked little savages to civilised youngsters with an urge to catch fish.

The hunting instinct that had belonged to our parents was strong, and we applied it to our own fishing. Our tackle was crude. Much of it had been handed down or secretly 'borrowed' from the head of the family, but with it we managed to learn the rudiments of casting and float control. We knew the best places to collect worms; we moulded paste from flour and stale bread, we stewed wheat in big iron pans and watched it with loving care until the precise moment when it split and became a soft and sweet-smelling bait for roach and dace. We devised devilish concoctions and secret baits which, in truth, were not as good as the simple ones that had stood the test of time. But from it all we devised means of catching the bream from Tring, the tench and rudd from Claydon, and the chub from the River Thame.

Still later, when we had learned the meaning of responsibility, we were allowed, as a special privilege, to fish occasionally for the big pike and tench in Wotton Lakes. That was, and indeed still is, a fisherman's paradise, not so much for the fish therein, but because the natural beauty still remains. Abstraction, pollution, and so-called progress have not yet encroached upon these beautiful waters. Please God, they never will!

It was there, at Wotton, that new methods, new techniques and improvements in fishing tackle were developed; and it was there that I began to take my fishing more seriously, but never so seriously that I failed to appreciate the beauties of nature and the wondrous changes that took place both in and around the water of this rather special fairyland.

I never caught a carp from Wotton, but I once found the body of what was apparently the largest wild, common carp ever recorded in this county, and I became stricken with carp fever. I had never wanted to fish at night, and I doubt if I ever would have, had it not been for the finding of that body. The immense pleasure of fishing at night can never adequately be described by the written word. It has to be practised to be understood, and there is no way of teaching it. It can only come from experience and a love of the waterside.

The whole scene changed at night. The small noises one would ignore by day are magnified a hundredfold by night. The rustlings of small creatures in the darkness bring to the fore deep-rooted instincts which do not exist by day. Trees cast weird shadows, snapping twigs cause the heart to beat faster, and the angler foolish enough to 'go it alone' might well be frightened into beating a hasty retreat! It has happened to me. The snortings of a badger have terrified me, and I have heard many strange and unaccountable noises in the dark hours. But I have learned that these things no longer exist when I am in the company of a good friend. Besides which, of course, much of the pleasure in night fishing comes in the quiet conversation with a good companion who shares my feelings as well as my mug of hot soup or freshly-brewed tea. There are more exciting ways of fishing, there are more active methods of fishing, and there are forms of fishing which require a deal more manual skill, but none is more rewarding or satisfying.

From these lessons at Wotton I learned to catch carp in other lakes, and how to catch barbel in waters farther afield, and I can claim moderate success with many other species both at home and abroad. But I am still learning and expect to go on learning, until I can no longer wield a fishing rod.

Today I have up-to-date equipment and sophisticated instruments to help me fish in vast waters that are not easily understood, and there have been times when I have wondered whether the simple pleasures I once enjoyed were lost forever in this wild pursuit of angling perfection.

Would I ever again revel in the sheer joy of catching small, unsophisticated fish that really required no angling skill? And now that I have modern camping, caravan and boat facilities, would the cooking of such small fish over an open fire be an anti-climax?

I need not have worried!

Up in the Rocky Mountains of Idaho a few years ago, two good friends and I made our camp. We didn't pitch tents, but cut a long pole with the axe to hold up the big canvas sheet which was our only shelter. We cut spruce, lodgepole pine and larch branches and made our 'bough beds' out of the springy twigs. We piled them up to a height of several feet and rolled on them until the piles were soft and flat. It all took time, but the beds were as sweet-smelling as new-mown hay, and they were so comfortable that we did not want to leave them. We built our fireplace with rocks, and we took turns to carry the water and do the camp chores.

We crawled out of our beds in the morning and hung up our frost-covered sleeping bags to thaw in the morning sun. We cooked our eggs and bacon in the big skillet over the open fire. We fished for the little brook trout and when we had caught enough, we brought them back to camp and cooked them. We baked potatoes in the embers, and we brewed tea in a soot-blackened pot. We wandered up and down the great basin and marvelled at the butterflies and birds of many colours like the blue jays that came and cleared away our edible refuse.

We followed tracks of beaver and we teased the pine squirrels that resented our presence. We watched the antelope and coyotes through the glasses and we never had time to do all we wanted to do. At night we stoked up the fire and sat and talked into the early morning hours and drank whisky diluted with the icy cold water of the mountain stream. And as the fire died we crawled into our beds by the light of the old lantern.

The wheel had turned full circle. It was as if I was back to the days of my youth in the Vale—fishing and living out of doors for the sheer joy of it. And it never rained.

FRED J. TAYLOR
1972

There are three sorts of country in the counties near London. The most prevalent is the near-country, that is to say places where fields survive among widely scattered houses and which are not quite suburb. South Buckinghamshire is an example. Much of Surrey is another. Then, secondly, there is consciously preserved country such as may be found in Sussex and which becomes National Park, this is often unproductive moorland and heath and belts of conifers. The third sort of country is the kind into which the Vale of Aylesbury falls. That is to say, it is real country where agriculture is a primary occupation, where the same families have lived for generations, where the farms and villages are the gradual growth of centuries, the new blending fairly comfortably with the old as it does in Soulbury and indeed in all the villages in the area.

The scenery here in North Buckinghamshire is the sort that Henry James described as 'unmitigated England'. Elms, oaks, ashes and sycamores, red brick farms, houses and barns, the brick varying from the dark brownish-red of Tudor brick through the dark red brick patterned with sanded headers (dark blue glazed bricks) popular in the eighteenth century, to the pale red and yellowish brick of the early nineteenth century, particularly on the Bedfordshire borders of the area. There are half-timbered cottages with brick infilling and in the western part of the area limestone cottages with brick quoins.

There is thatch for roofing as well as tiles and slates. It is all unpretentious village building. The roads between the villages wind and climb, the prospects vary every few yards. Considering how near to London, it is amazing what wide prospects there are of trees and broad vales. It is the scenery that inspired William Cowper and John Milton.

I visited all the villages recently having not seen them since 1948, and found them surprisingly little changed, and where new houses had been introduced I could see that with time they will be part of the pattern of each village. The least spoiled was Dunton whose church is one of the very few churches in Buckinghamshire to escape Victorian 'restoration', at any rate so far as the nave is concerned. It has box pews, clear glass and a west gallery. It has the vestige of a village green and attractive Georgian and Tudor brick houses, sycamores and an unfenced road. The village of Hoggeston, a mile north-west of it, is really one of the best villages in Buckinghamshire, so far as the eye is concerned. Cublington, with its red brick and thatch, is the sort of village one would give a prize to as undisturbed England. The long street which is the village of Stewkley is a true story of the growth of nine centuries. Its Norman church is one of the few complete tripartite churches in England and was most sympathetically restored by George Edmund Street in the last century. Wing is another varied village with more to show even than Stewkley, and it has a Saxon church of unique plan and impressive splendour of proportion. To go to the western part of the area, Whitchurch is singularly unspoiled, despite the fact that a main road runs through it. Its church is medieval, stately and enormous. The village is full of old cottages and what looks like large farms or small manor houses; it has winding streets and trees and garden walls. In fact, I am not sure that it isn't the best village of the lot.

It is no good though, thinking of these churches and villages and country houses only as buildings worthy of preservation. One has to think of them in terms of people, too. They are part of the lives not only of the people but everybody in the neighbourhood who knows this part of Buckinghamshire, and with the growth of Aylesbury, Bletchley and the new town of Milton Keynes, it is a vital bit of real country for relaxation from the noise of industrialised urban life and the bleakness of planned dormitory towns. One cannot assess in terms of cash, or exports and imports, an imponderable thing like the turn of a lane or an inn or a church tower, or a familiar sky line.

Just try driving, as I did, with the wind behind you, and a western sun, on the leaves of elms and oaks, along the pleasant undulations from Winslow via Swanbourne, Drayton Parslow and Hollingdon to Soulbury, and you will see what I mean.

SIR JOHN BETJEMAN
Bucks Life, August 1970

> Your hands, my dear adorable,
>   Your lips of tenderness
> —Oh, I've loved you faithfully and well,
>   Three years, or a bit less.
>   It wasn't a success.
>
> Thank God that's done! and I'll take the road,
>   Quit of my youth and you,
> The Roman road to Wendover
>   By Tring and Lilley Hoo,
>   As a free man may do.
>
> For youth goes over, the joys that fly
>   The tears that follow fast;
> And the dirtiest things we do must lie
>   Forgotten at the last;
>   Even Love goes past.
>
> What's left behind I shall not find,
>   The splendour and the pain;
> The splash of sun, the shouting winds,
>   And the brave sting of rain,
>   I may not meet again.
>
> But the years, that take the best away,
>   Give something in the end;
> And a better friend than love have they,
>   For none to mar or mend,
>   That have themselves to friend.

RUPERT BROOKE
'The Chilterns',
The Collected Poems, 1918

Enigma

> Some foreigners find it confusing
> To visit the County of Bucks;
> They've expected to hear
> There are vast herds of deer,
> Or see flocks of Aylesbury ducks!
>
> RUTH REYNOLDS

One evening in May I took the path across Aylesbury Common to Bishopstone. Though so near to the county town – a matter of only a mile and a half as the crow flies – this village preserves its rural character as tenaciously as any in the county. The reason is not far to seek for during rainy weather the path in many places becomes waterlogged and the cart roads which one has to traverse are almost impassable with mud; besides, the stiles are high, and present an insurmountable difficulty to many. In addition to these disadvantages, the high roads leading to it, the first by the Bugle Horn at Hartwell, and the other through Stoke Mandeville, make such wide detours that they place the village beyond the reach of a comfortable and gentle walk; thus it is that only during the summer months it is visited by the few who venture across the fields.

It was one of those occasions when casually entering a remote inn, I stumbled upon one of those old villagers with a vivid recollection of the events that took place locally years ago. In the evenings when their daily toil is ended, they are found taking their rest, sometimes with their bread and cheese in one hand, a pocket knife in the other and an onion on the taproom table, enjoying what is locally known as a 'thumb-bit'. Then in the quiet and friendly atmosphere of the inn, they become expansive and readily relate their experiences, both of the present and of former days; also, when they feel a mutual sympathy and interest are present, their joys and sorrows too. It was not long before I joined in the talk, which was principally on casual subjects, such as the weather, crops, and the comparison of the present time with the past.

The conversation then turned on to the discoveries made in the Anglo-Saxon burial ground just beyond the village, and then to the belief in witches and ghosts that prevailed years ago.

'Everybody believed in ghosts and witches then,' he said, 'but we don't hear much about them in these days. Many people don't believe in them, but there are still some who say they are to be seen today. Years ago there used to be women (witches) who would bewitch cattle, and do all sorts of things. I heard my father say that when he was a young man he used to go to Oxford and bring back a load of coal. Whenever he was just opposite a house this side of Wheatley his horses shivered and shook like aspens, and he had the hardest job to get them by the spot. He could not make out why they did this, until he was told an old witch lived there, and she had done the same to many other teams. I can't disbelieve my own father, and that is what he told me.

'Then there used to be those little witches that used to get about the fields, sitting on gates, and on the hurdles of sheepfolds. Sometimes when a shepherd went to look at his fold of sheep he would see every one of them looking up, and not one a-feeding, and all had got their heads turned in one direction. As he got nearer he would see a funny looking little man sitting on the top bar of one of the hurdles, with a body something in the shape of a toy balloon, with long legs and a pickid nose; and there he sat making all sorts of faces at the sheep. When he was doing that they could not take their eyes off him. When the shepherd got close to the fold the old witch would shout: "Hippy! Hippy! over the hedge I go!" and off he would gallop on the hurdle across the field and jump over the hedge, just like the wind. Then the sheep would start feeding again, and the shepherd would see no more of him for some time. After a while, when least expected, he would be seen again, perhaps on a gate or hurdle, and go through the same performance. I never saw one of this kind myself, but I did see something one morning which was either a witch or a ghost, and this is how it happened.

'Some years ago, in the dark days, just before it was light, I fetched my horse out of the stable, and took it to the cart to shut it in. When I tried to back it into the shafts it would not go in, but shivered and shook from head to foot, so that I could not understand what was the matter with it. All at once I happened to turn round in the way the horse was facing, and then I saw, about a dozen yards or so in front, one of the funniest looking things as ever I did see in all my life. It was something like an old ram, but bigger. It kept still for a minute or so, then it began to move about, first on one side and then on the other, and at last it slunk away in the darkness.

In the meantime other villagers had entered for their evening's diversion, and there was a nice company present by the time our conversation ceased. However, I stayed but a little while longer, for looking out of the window I saw the sun resting on the horizon; so rising from my seat and wishing the company 'Goodnight', I left, and proceeded on my way home across the fields.

A few weeks later I was passing through Marsh, having walked from Kimble. Reaching the little witchert cottage where the road bends, I proceeded on my way towards Bishopstone through the avenue of tall elms, and approached the three little cottages by the side of the road, just beyond. As I got near the second, an old countryman whom I had spoken to on previous occasions when I had passed that way, looked over his garden hedge, and said: 'I thaht twas you; ye ant bin this way fur some time now, a ye? I caught sight an ye as ye were a-comin up the rooad. How be ye?' 'Very well,' I replied, 'and how are you?' 'I be a bit better than what e was when you last see me. Be ye a-comin in fur a few minutes?'

I went up to the gate, opened it, and walked up the garden path. The cottage had been newly white-washed, and the little tin plate which was fastened just above the porch was splashed from one side to the other, but I could still decipher the name written upon it: ROSEBINE COTTAGE. It required some little effort to read the characters, but they were plain enough when once distinguished. Very homely and artless the inscription looked, but yet in perfect harmony with the environment. We entered the house and sat by the fire, as living alone, he had been doing a little cooking.

'This is a lovely place in summer,' I said, 'but I suppose tis a bit dark and lonely in winter.'

'Ah, begoy! tis a bit, but e dooant git out much then. I can't walk like e used to.'

'Is this house in Kimble or in Stone Parish?'

'Kimbul; the boundary runs acrass jest bi the carner; a little furder up.'

'There's a nice piece of wasteland by the sides of the road.'

'Yes, I used to have a pigsty an the bank, jest past the house, and I reeard a good many fat hogs in it, but e pulled it down some time agoo. I a lived in this house awf and on all mi life; mi father built it about ninety yeeurs agoo. The thetched one on tuther side is built a witchert dug up from a feeuld down in Mash. We dooant git much company, and I dooant know as e wants it now-a-deeahs. When I was a young man the gipsies used to camp jest up bi the geeat. They were alwiz about in they days. Ole Critty Smith was one who used to be heeur. They ood stop a little while and then be awf. When one lot was gone anothur come along. One an em axed me to marry his dahter, and then goo about the country wi him in the boxin booths, but when mi mother heeurd an it she went an so alarmingly, that nothing nivver come an it. We nivver got interrupted bi any an em, but ye had to look out fur yu-ur things, as they ood lay ther hands an anything as they could claa holt an. Ye could nivver git the better an em in dealin fur they were the cunningest people as ivver e had anything to do wi. They all knowed me and so e got an purty well wi em, but thaiur was one ole diddicoy as done me out a two pounds. That was in Wycombe, one markut day. I went over as usual to teeak mi eggs, fur I was eggler about heeur then, and went to the White Hart wheeur e alwiz put up. As soon as ivver I got thaiur this old diddicoy come up wi a harse and axed me to buy it. He trotted it up and down the straat jest to show its peeaces and then kep an axin me to buy. I could see twant no good, and so e toald him that e dint want it; besides I dint want anothur as the one I got sarved me quite well. Howivver, when he found he coont meeak me buy, he come up to me and says: "I can trust you wi two hunderd pounds! Hold out yu-ur hands!" I hilt out mi hands and putting his hand in his pockets he pulled out five bags a money. He put a bag in aich a mi hands, one an the top a mi head, and one an aich a mi shelders. "Now," he says, "I can trust you wi two hunderd pounds." I said, "I dooant belaive thair's two hunderd pounds in they bags." "All right," he says, "we ull see!" He opened one, and took out forty golden sovereigns, and counted ivvery one in front a me. Then he says: "Do ye belaive it now?" "Yes," I says. So wi that he put all the bags in his pockuts. "Now," he says, "you see I trusted you wi two hunderd pounds; now you trust me wi a couple a pounds fur a little while." I took out a couple uv pounds and put one in aich of his hands as he was a-holdin out to me. He then went to his harse and agen started runnin him up and down the streeat, and ivvery now and agen axin me whether I ood buy. He had done this a good few times when I could see he was teeakin longer runs than he did at fust. At the end a one a the runs, when they were neeurly at the bottom a the streeat, a man standin behind me said, "Thaiur's somebody wants to spaik to ye inside at once.' So I went in the taproom to see who it was, and found nobody was thaiur as wanted to spaik to me. I come out at once, but begoy! I found the ole diddicoy was no-wheeur to be sin – he had bolted wi mi money. I run down the streeat to find him, but he was gone, and I coont tell which way he went.

'Howivver, I met a man as I knowed, and so I axed him whether he had sin any gipsies. "Yes," he says, "I see em a-gooin down tords the Rye as fast as they could goo." I went back to the White Hart, got mi harse and followed. As I went along I kep axin peepul if they had sin em, and they told me they waunt fur in front. As I got near Ooburn Green I could see em ahead, but they cotch sight a me fust and I could jest see the ole diddicoy as had got mi money gooin acrass a meddur as fast as he could, wheeur I coont follur him, and leaving tuthers to feeace it out.

'When I reached em I jumped out a mi cart, and claad holt a the harse as the old rogue had tried to sell me, but all the tuthers come round and said the harse waunt hisn but twas theirn. I told em how e had bin dizzled out a the two pounds, but they woont belaive it, and as they had begun to git a bit rusty, I had to leeav em and git back, fur I coont a fout the whool packut an em.

'I dint see him fur a couple uv yeeurs artur that, but one day when I was in Wycombe, I happund to see him. I knowed him as soon as ivver I see him, so I went straight up to him and said, "You be the man as bolted wi they two pounds a mine two yeeurs agoo." "No," said the ole diddicoy, "I baint the man; twas mi brother. You maiad a mistaiak." "I be sure an it," I says. "Then you be wrong," he says, "fur I know it was mi brother as he toald me he had done it." I found twas no good a-spaikin to him about it, so artur a time he said, "Come and have a drink." So he went to the White Hart and had it, but I took gallus good ceear I dint trait him. Artur a while I left and come gently an hooam to Bishton.'

The conversation then drifted to other subjects.

B. 'I reckon this was a place where there used to be ghosts once on a time.'

A. 'Ah, begoy! I a heeurd mi father spaik about em but I a nivver sin one. They saimed to be about when he was alive, but peepul dooant belaive in em now. He tooald me when he was a bo-ey as thaiur was a ole ooman as lived in Bishton and she was a witch. She'd got a son – a big strong bo-ey as she had leeat in life. One day she took him out into a meddur wheeur there were some hurduls. She went and picked one up, stroddled acrass it, and gallupd round the meddur like the wind. When she was a comin back and got neeur him she had to jump ovur a bruck. She went over it like a reeas-harse. As soon as the lad see her do it, he shouted out, "Well jumped, mother!" At once the ole witch stopped and could goo no furdur. She let the 'urdle fall to the ground, and walking up to him says: "When I be a-doin sich things as these, ye mahnt spaik, fur when ye do the spell's broke. Tha's it; ye mahnt spaik ur meeak a noise, if ye do, they witches be done and can't goo an."

'Did you ever see those little witches that went about the fields?' I enquired.

'No, I nivver, but begoy! I a sin they little people as dances about in the moonlight.'

'Where was that?'

'At Eethrup down an the lawn. Some yeeurs agoo I was night watchman down at Eethrup House, and ivvery night from twelve o'clock to one in the mornin I had to be at the pavilion. I alwiz had a good big dog wi me in ceeas e met any porchers ur see anybody a-prowlin about. I hand't bin thaiur very long when one night as the moon was gettin an tords full, and I was a-standin under some laurels so that nobody could see me, I heeurd sich a rustlin about in the leevs. I took no no-atice an it as e thought twas ony a lot a rabbuts a-scamperin about, but th' ole dog kept an a-growlin and tuggin at his cheean. At last I meead him kaip quiet, but it waunt fur long as he started agen, and would kaip an, so e thought e ood have a look to see what the row was about. I went up to the edge uv the bush and looked wheeur the noise was a-comin frum, and begoy! what e thought was rabbuts were little men, the funniest lookin little cocks as ivver I did see. I dinno what to meeak an em, I could hardly belaive mi own eyes. I nivver did see sich gooins-an. They were all an a opun speeace an the ground wheeur the moonlight shone through the trais. I could see ivvery one an em as pleean as daylight and e stood and looked at em fur ivver so long, and they nivver took a bit a noatice a me ur mi dog, though some an en come quite neeur the bush. They danced and jumped and cee-aperd (capered) all round the pleeace and pulled sich funny feeaces as I coont kaip mi eyes awf em. I looked at em fur some time and when it was time fur me to goo I left em a-gooin-an jest like they did when e fust see em.'

'Did you ever see them again?'

'Plenty a times, but alwiz an moonlight nights. Sometimes they got an the lawn.'

'How big were they?'

'Not very big . . . not quite half the height uv yu-ur walkin-stick. They got big heads as saimed too heavy fur their bodies, sich funny little eyes, long pickid noo-azes and sich long feeaces as they ood pull about in all mannur a

Rooks' nests in the elms between Chilton and Brill.

ways. They all wore short jackuts and had got ony very short thighs, but very long thin legs so that they saimed to be all legs, and when they stood still ivvery one saimed knocked-knaid (kneed); but, begoy! when they muv about they run like lightning. I a heeurd they come out a the cellur a the old house as was pulled down yeeurs agoo, but e ant heeurd as anybody a sin em fur yeeurs now. Eethrup used to be a very funny pleeace. I knowed a man, neeamed Adams as was walkin down the hill in bright moonlight, and when he got a little way down he was overtook bi a gret tall man wearin a high baiver hat and a long coo-at. Ole Adams a begun a-spaikin to him and talked to him moast a the way down, but the man nivver answered a wurd. When they got an a bit furder ole Adams says, "Master, thaiur's some fine cattul in this heeur meddur, come and have a look at em." So he walked up to the geeat, expectin the man to follur him, but when he turned round the man was nowheeur to be sin. He looked up the hill and down it, but nobody was in sight, so when he got hooam he su-ur he had sin a ghooast. I ixpect these ghooast-es and little devils, as I call em, had summut to do wi Lord Stanhope when he lived at Eethrup House. I nivver did see a ghoo-ast miself, but I had a bit uv a fright one dark night gooin acrass a meddur. I had jest got about to the middul when a white form stood streeat in front a me. Mi hair saimed to stand bolt upright, and jest fur a minute I was sceeard out a mi senses. Howivver, e thaht, "I baint afeeard uv any man, and I wunt be afeeard a that." So I walked on and found it was ony a cow as muv out a mi way when e got clooas to't.'

The conversation then ended. Picking up my hat I prepared to leave. 'Which way be ye a-gooin?' he says. 'If ye want a short cut ye ood better goo bi Standall's and acrass the feeulds.'

'I think I shall go back Stoke way for I have plenty of time,' I rejoined.

H. HARMAN
Sketches of the Bucks Countryside, 1934

Our Farm. I live on a farm. The farm is at Dorton. On the farm there is a barn. The rats run about and make Mum shout. It is a big farm. We have 50 pigs, 50 calves and 300 chickens. We have two rams and two bulls. All of them have horns. One of the rams has a bad leg so he cannot chase us. But the others can.

Ludgershall Gazette, Vol. I, 1961
produced by the children of the
C. of E. Primary School, Ludgershall

We do not sell our secrets like
The other shires try to do.
And those bred here alone will find
The secrets of the chosen few.
Nor Bideford, nor Parracombe,
Nor Dart, nor Devon's Plymouth Hoe;
But plain, ungarnished Luggershaw,
Marsh Gibbon, Brill and Hampden Row;
For Exe and Teign and Culm and Tawe
And cream and cider, tor and hoe
Are only common property
For anyone to see and know,
But the lips of the men of Bucks alone
By Chiltern air are purified.
The barren breasts of Ivinghoe,
And ridge and bottom are their guide.
We find it hard to worship pike,
Crag, dale, moor, moss and lonely fell;
For Great and Little, ham, ton, den,
Low, end and green have cast their spell.
No secret lies in Striding Edge,
Great Gable, Coniston Old Man,
But Boddington, Coombe Hill and Kop
Shall hoard the song our hearts began.

No Stickletarn, no Bassenthwaite,
No Cumberland or Appleby –
The Thames, the Ouse, the Chess, the Thame,
Are waters good enough for me.
Llanberis, Barmouth, Bala, coed,
Cwm, afon, moel, fach and llyn
For them. For us, the Icknield Way,
Where the plain ends and the woods begin.
The chalk in this, our native land,
Was scattered with a liberal hand.
The holly hedges, massive, tall
And changeless, stand from fall to fall;
And in our words, the cherry trees
Blossom forth just when they please.
Along the milk-and-honey Vale
Shall the broken speech of Bucks prevail,
Rushing, like an all-cleansing stream
Our thoughts go where the bloodstones gleam.
Fresh flints will come to our poor eyes
Glittering under Chiltern skies.
Like the sure, deep throb of a distant train
Our history echoes in my brain;
So, when our woods, the vale, have gone
This shall remain, surpassed by none.

H. EVELYN HOWARD
'My County'
Quoted in *Landmarks*,
edited by Hamilton & Arlott, 1943

On the night of 8th January 1921, Lord and Lady Lee of Fareham entertained several leading statesmen at dinner: Lloyd George, the then Prime Minister, Lord Reading, Sir Robert Horne and Sir Hamar Greenwood. When the meal was over the hosts bade farewell to their guests – but with an unprecedented turn of custom. For it was the hosts themselves who entered their car and drove away. Thus unobtrusively did the house known as Chequers become a gift to the nation.

The history of the Lee family has long been one of altruistic service to the country, and of long association with the Vale of Aylesbury. In the National Gallery hangs a picture of Queen Elizabeth I, surrounded by her courtiers, one of whom is Sir Henry Lee, K.G., her Champion. Sir Henry was the Lord of Fleet Marston and Quarrendon; he lived (and is buried) in Quarrendon Manor. In 1592, with due pomp and ceremony, he entertained his

Queen at his country seat. Sir Henry was also a man with advanced ideas about education from which Aylesbury was later to benefit, as he was the founder of the Aylesbury Free School.

Lady Margaret Lee, mother of Sir Henry, lies buried in St Peter's Chapel at Quarrendon Manor. Lady Margaret was the heiress of Hardwicke where yet more Lees are commemorated on a wall plaque in the village church. On this plaque Sir Robert and Lady Lee kneel facing each other, with rows of sons and daughters kneeling behind them.

The Lee connection with Chequers began before the First World War when Lord and Lady Lee of Fareham were searching for a country cottage in the neighbourhood of the Vale. In the course of their search they came across a forlorn Elizabethan house in a sheltered hollow of the Chiltern Hills near Ellesborough. Neglected as it was, its possibilities were apparent, and the Lees thereupon determined to make its restoration their hobby.

During the First World War they turned Chequers into a convalescent hospital which was staffed and equipped at their own expense. It was shortly after this time that they decided to give the house to the nation as a thanksgiving for England's deliverance, and as a 'place of rest and recreation for Prime Ministers forever'. In the wording of the trust, Lord Lee hopes that 'the antiquity and calm tenacity of Chequers and its annals might suggest some saving virtues in the continuity of English history and exercise a check upon too hasty upheavals, whilst even the most reactionary (statesman) could scarcely be insensible to the spirit of human freedom which permeates the countryside of Hampden, Burke and Milton.'

From the Library of the
Friends of the Vale of Aylesbury

QUAINTON CHURCHYARD

I kneel in sunlight, lifting to a stone
A hand made sensitive to joy and pain,
This instrument of scarlet and warm bone,
To learn the sorrow a few words contain,
And pick at the vanished capitals in the stone:
Nerves upon sunlit emptiness, in vain.
   Only a cherub looks into the air
   Keeping the secret from me without guile:
   He has forgotten why his lips still wear
   The obliterated sweetness of a smile.
The burning stone against my finger tips
Is only burning stone for all they do,
   They never will come nearer to
The sorrow that informed those smiling lips.

Yet must I call, though mutely, grope and call,
Saying, Consumptive by the neighbours heard
All one Winter coughing in the wall,
Or Child, perhaps, with breast-bone of a bird,
Bones that were once, and then forever, small –
Whoever's lost in this green, natured word –
    Listen! for one is kneeling to you, one
    But for the slant of time most like to you:
    You in the shadow, he yet in the sun.
    If I should know one commonest thing you knew –
The eye of evening blue on house and hill –
The shuffling of a collie on a chain
    Who stretches into sleep again –
Speak to me, ghost, in burning England still!

A whisper out of nowhere, born between
The shadows and the tumble of the rose,
Touches my hand – as though I had not seen
How beautiful is evening when it grows
Into a pencilled profile, how serene
The face of death, how lasting the repose.
    But someone brought into a world with crying,
    To wake and dream and call it once his own,
    This which I cannot waken with my prying,
    A little sad brown hair and dreamless bone.
The whisper grows among the luminous boughs,
Till all the silks of Summer are unfurled –
    I rise in rapture to my world,
And Summer's like a laurel round my brows.

LAURENCE WHISTLER
The World's Room, The Collected Poems, 1949

At Stage V[1] there was a picture on the wall of the corridor of the Piccadilly Hotel – a reproduction of a painting of the Vale by Rex Whistler. This, as I passed and re-passed it day after day, helped to form my view. . . . It was as potent as any of the evidence I heard. The Chiltern escarpment, from Ivinghoe Beacon to Beacon Hill by Watlington, the Vale, and the low-rise hills beyond at Cublington, Whitchurch, Oving and Quainton, seem to me to form an entity every bit as valuable as the North and South Downs with the Weald in between. The view north-westwards from the Chilterns is as rewarding as any in the south of England; and the view from the Vale in the reverse direc-

[1] Of the deliberations of the Roskill Commission.

Dorton House, which now houses Ashfold Preparatory School was begun on the site of an earlier house by Sir John Dormer in 1596, the year in which he served as High Sheriff of Buckinghamshire, and was finished in 1626. The house is in the shape of a Roman H, and encloses three sides of a courtyard. The architect is unknown. The building is of Gothic shape with Classical decoration, Tudor chimneys and mullions. One of its main features is the saloon which contains a fine Jacobean screen, and the original fireplace and panelling. In 1783 the house was sold to Sir John Aubrey whose coat of arms appears above the fireplace. On the first floor is an Elizabethan room containing the original ceiling, panelling, and carved Jacobean overmantel.

tion is exactly the one that attracted Whistler. The ridge road from Whitchurch through Oving and Pitchcott to Waddesdon is as beautiful a road (for its views) as any I know in the home counties. Time and time again since the end of Stage V, I have recalled Mr Niall McDermott's words in his closing address when he remarked that anyone standing on one of the famous vantage points of the Chilterns and looking out over the Vale of Aylesbury would say, 'It simply is unthinkable that an airport and all it implies should be brought here.'

. . . It is a snug, homely and very livable part of the world. It has been occupied for several thousand years, and as a result it has an extraordinary wealth of associations – historical, architectural and literary. The work of previous generations can be seen on every hand – from Iron Age forts, ancient trackways, Roman roads, and the complete spectrum of ecclesiastical, military and domestic architecture. It is of great interest geologically, with the chalk strata of the Chilterns dipping under London, coming up again in the North Downs, descending (the over-arch having been eroded away) to form the South Downs. The southern limits of the ice-sheet can be traced across the area. It still possesses a great richness of flora and fauna in spite of pollution and insecticides. It is full of treasures – great houses, fine gardens, immaculate villages, art collections and museums. It still has the softest and subtlest landscapes to be found anywhere in the world, landscapes which have inspired generations of English poets and painters.

For decades it has been the policy of successive governments to conserve this part of the country. There has been no dispute about it. The effort has been largely successful in spite of intense pressures for urbanisation, industrial development, dumping of waste, exploitation of minerals, extraction of timber, the rapidly changing pattern of agriculture (which, paradoxically, probably presents the greatest threat of all to the English countryside), new roads, pollution in many forms, and the exigencies of two wars which have left their litter of camps, depots, airfields and hard-standings under the cover of woodlands. In spite of these the area remains miraculously more or less intact – playground for thousands, refuge for those who seek quiet and solitude, chock-full of things to do and things to be interested in, the envy of our Australian, New Zealand and American cousins.

. . . I believe, as I have said before, that the Vale of Aylesbury is a critically important part of this island. It is part of the fundamental hill and dale, forest and farmland break between London and Birmingham. It is of immense value to the nation, even more so to my mind than the Nuthampstead area which lies on the fringe of an unbroken stretch of countryside extending northwards throughout East Anglia to the sea. To locate the airport squarely athwart the break between the country's two largest conurbations, with the noise area extending from south-west to north-east for nearly forty miles, and with the consequent constraint on all the modest activities that the area so conveniently accommodates at present and all those that it could accommodate in future, would seem to me to constitute nothing less than an environmental disaster. SIR COLIN BUCHANAN

The Note of Dissent,
18th December 1970

It is wholly fitting and right that this great fight should have taken place over the Vale of Aylesbury. History may say that it was the turning-point at which the people rose against arbitrary planning and destruction of their way of life. It may be that the tide of national opinion was already flowing in that direction; but the tremendous resistance of the people sparked off the decision, for the first time, to create a Ministry for the Environment. One of the results of this is the saving for England of this living community unsurpassed in its expression of what is known the world over as 'the English way of life'.

DESMOND FENNELL
for WARA during the Third London Airport Controversy,
1969–71

Dunton Church.

In the little Church of Dunton with its box pews, gallery and medieval roof timbers there is an inscription which reads:

'For 800 years successive generations have met here to offer the sacrifice of praise and thanksgiving and to pray for themselves and others to your heavenly Father... You stand on Holy ground, hallowed by ages of Christian worship.'

Those to whose lot it fell to demolish these churches would stand on such holy ground, as, indirectly, would those who had to order their demolition. In these and in every parish church in the county are the names of the men who in two world wars gave their lives defending, as they thought, their familiar homes and fields. In some cases they numbered half the adult population of the village. They fought and died that England, as they knew it, might endure and be saved from destruction, and that the Englishman's traditional freedom from tyranny and arbitrary injustice won by their forefathers should be preserved for their posterity.

SIR ARTHUR BRYANT
*Extract from evidence set before the
Roskill Commission, 1970*

The exact limits of the Vale of Aylesbury cannot be drawn, for there are no clear-cut boundaries, either geographical or political. Leland, in his *Itinerary*, 1540, states: 'The Vale goeth one waye to the Forrest beyond Tame Market. It goeth other wayes to Buckingham, to Stoneye Stratford; to Newport Pagnell, and alonge from Aylesbury by the rootes of the Chiltern Hilles almost to Dunstable.' Three centuries later Dr George Lipscomb in his *County History*, 1847, describes it thus: 'The town (Aylesbury) imparts its name to the large and fruitful Vale of Aylesbury, long celebrated for verdure and fertility, its corn and cattle; extending from the foot of the Chiltern Hills and the western border of Hertfordshire towards the north, to Wingrave and Oving, is skirted by the hills of Quainton and Pitchcott, and stretches westwards almost to the verge of Oxfordshire, losing its appellation in the track of woodland formerly Bernwode-Forest.' In the present day Sir Arthur Bryant in his preface to this book offers a more concise definition, particularly as to what constitutes the 'heart' of the Vale; it is by these three authors that we have been guided in compiling the following directory of villages. Our selection should not be understood as a further attempt to define the limits of the area; we are aware that some of the villages listed cannot be said to lie within the Vale proper. Rather, our aim has been to express more fully its character by including those neighbouring villages that are linked to the Vale by a common spirit, historical association, or, in some cases simply by offering a wider visual outlook across its tranquil landscape.

Ascott has a timber-framed house, partly dated 1606 but considerably enlarged since it was purchased by Leopold de Rothschild in 1874. One of the National Trust's great assets on the edge of the Vale, Ascott's fine collection of pictures and its gardens, now open to the public, bring many visitors from all over the world.

Ashendon straddles a hill offering a magnificent view to the four corners of the Vale. The old Bakehouse and Red Lion Inn cluster below the church, which has been well restored. There is a blocked Norman doorway and, among other interesting features, the effigy of a knight of the late thirteenth century.

Askett, below the slope of the Chiltern Hills looking across the flat stretches of the Vale, is a small collection of houses typical of the area, built of thatch, brick and witchert (dried clay, plastered and colour-washed).

***Aston Abbots** has a fine position between gated roads in rolling countryside and was formerly a property belonging to Abbots of St Albans. The thin Perpendicular tower of the church dominates the village. Note the mid-Victorian window, dedicated to Sir James Clark Ross, who discovered the magnetic pole in 1831. His portrait appeared on a stamp in 1972.

***The 'Doomed Villages'**. Cublington, Aston Abbots, Dunton, Soulbury, Stewkley, Wing and Whitchurch were referred to as the 'Doomed Villages' during the fight against the siting of the Third London Airport at Wing.

Aston Clinton is a Rothschild village; the Gothic school near the church was a gift in 1856. Today the Bell inn brings visitors from all over the world who appreciate fine cuisine. The church has been restored with fluctuating zeal, in fact the bowl of the Norman font was once reduced to service as a garden urn. In the churchyard lie many members of the Lake family whose manor once stood on this spot.

Aston Sandford. Of the rectory Sir John Betjeman says in a letter: 'It is nice to be writing to the *very house* where Thomas Scott lived, author of the *Force of Truth* (a great book) friend of Cowper and Newton, grandfather of Sir Gilbert Scott, converter of Newman to Calvinism in his youth.' The Rev. Thomas Scott lived in Aston Sandford from 1800 to 1821 and died there. He was founder of the Church Missionary Society, wrote a six-volume commentary on the Bible, published many sermons and discourses and was a great preacher, so popular that he preached out of a 'window' to a tent erected in the churchyard.

The small church (with wooden bell tower) has a thirteenth-century Christ-figure in stained glass above the altar, reputed to have been brought to Aston Sandford for safety. It also has a modern window designed and executed by Michael Farrar Bell of Haddenham, in memory of Reginald Good, 1897–1964, who lived at the Manor and farmed there. Sir G. Gilbert Scott designed the manor house in brick and stone, and manor cottage in the same style. During World War II the Tithe Barn was used as a billiards room for RAF men stationed in Haddenham.

Aylesbury, the County Town. Once a market town for the area, it has now grown to contain many light industries as well. The Church of St Mary, built on the site of a Saxon church, is Early English, and has a fine west doorway. The tower was restored in 1805 and can be seen from many roads in the Vale, but it is now overshadowed by Mr Pooley's towering County Office building which from the distance looks rather like a fortress. In the church there is a Norman font, and Saxon crypt below the Lady Chapel, but probably the Monument of Lady Lee in the north transept, a fine piece of Elizabethan sculpture brought from the ruined church at Quarrendon, will be of more interest; her descendants gave Chequers to the nation as a retreat for the Prime Minister.

In Church Street is the County Museum; its collection is of great value especially to archaeologists. This is located in the centre of the small section of the 'old town', which is fortunately being preserved. The open market that had been held for centuries in the old square has now been removed to the new shopping complex including a splendid library and a multi-storey car park, which H.R.H. Princess Margaret opened on 14th July 1970. H.R.H. Princess Alexandra opened the College of Further Education on 18th July 1963, and the High School on 20th May 1960. H.R.H. The Duchess of Kent attended the Annual Conference of the British Legion (Women's Section) here on 20th November 1968.

Hazell's printing works (Hazell, Watson & Viney Ltd) were among the first undertakings to move to Aylesbury from London. Today they are known all over the world for their production of such famous publications as the *Reader's Digest*, the *R.A.C. Guide*, very many Penguins and other paperbacks. Colonel Oscar Viney has been a great benefactor to Aylesbury in preserving the old centre of the town.

Her Majesty Queen Elizabeth II paid a Royal Visit to the county on 6th April 1962. H.R.H. The Duke of Edinburgh, who visited Aylesbury on 13th July 1958, arrived by helicopter on Hazell's sports field.

Bierton is now a continuation of Aylesbury on a busy main road and few people stop to visit the early fourteenth-century Church of St James, with its crossing tower. Also typical of that century are the tall arcades, with their quatrefoil piers and many moulded capitals. There is a simple Norman font, and a monument, dated 1621, with small kneeling figures. Near the church is an early seventeenth-century cottage of brick and timber, and a house with picturesque gables.

Bishopstone is so called because it was one of the manors presented by William the Conqueror to his half-brother Bishop Odo. Saxon relics have been found here.

Bledlow-cum-Saunderton presents a fine view from the Chilterns across the Vale. The Norman church is the background for a 'Son et Lumiere', local voices giving the long history of the village. A Roman-British villa was found between Cuttlebrook and Wainhill, and on the Cop were found relics of the Bronze Age and Saxon period. Bledlow Cross is cut in chalk on the slopes of Wainhill. There are pleasant cottages and houses, and a visit to the Red Lion would be most rewarding.

Boarstall, stands in a formerly thickly wooded neighbourhood extending into Oxfordshire, once part of Bernwood forest; a remote village famous as the site of Boarstall castle. This was a Royalist stronghold during the Civil War, but now nothing remains but the moat and tower gateway. Myth has it that the name commemorates an enormous boar slain by a certain Nigel in the time of Edward the Confessor. As a reward the King gave him rights over the locality, with duties to protect the King's game. A horn presented as a symbol of this lease is kept in the archives at Aylesbury. His descendants have held the mansion of Boarstall ever since, but in 1943 it was given to the National Trust by Mr E. E. Cook. The great gateway enables us to picture Boarstall Castle in the days gone by. The old Duck Decoy, restored under the auspices of WAGBI, can be visited daily except Mondays.

Brill has a character all its own. It is almost entirely in terracotta brick with splashes of white, which gives it a very orderly appearance. The Green, War Memorial and the Square are the three centres, with roads leading to superb views over all sides of the Vale. The modern houses beside the old Post Office harmonise well. The church is full of interest: there is also a team of bellringers. Pottery from the fourteenth-century kiln near Temple Farm can be seen; brick and tile-making continued to be local industries until recently. Nearby is Muswell Hill, described by Sir Arthur Bryant as giving the finest view in southern England within fifty miles of London. Windmill Hill provides a fine picnic place.

Buckland Church is one of the few churches in Buckinghamshire in the gift of the Queen, and celebrates its 700th anniversary in 1973. It is mostly Victorian but has a thirteenth-century fluted font and a fourteenth-century doorway. Buckland was a village of straw-plaiters, the work then being sent to Luton for hat-making. The Grand Junction Canal once brought a great deal of work, and entries in the church records show that many of the inhabitants were engaged in this activity.

Chearsley. The village at one time produced lace, and pins and needles. The church, which was a chapel-at-ease served by the monks of Notley Abbey until the Dissolution, has a rough beam roof and modern box-pews which were copied from the originals by Ivor Newton, wood carver of Haddenham. The two front pews are in memory of Sir Henry Floyd, a former Lord Lieutenant of the County, whose name is also gratefully remembered by the county at the Floyd Auditorium at Stoke Mandeville Hospital and a school in Aylesbury. The font is dated 1250. A stump in the churchyard was probably the village cross, sometimes called Butter Cross, where local people sold their farm produce. A small house near the Green called the Boot may have been originally a pilgrim's hostel (*cf* North Marston). Lower Green Farmhouse is fifteenth or sixteenth century.

Cheddington. In this farming area one can still see on the slopes of Westend and Southend hills the terracing of primitive field systems, called 'lynchets'.

Chilton House, in rose brick, was built *circa* 1740 on a model of Buckingham House in London (*cf* Wotton). It provides one of the finest views over the Vale. The village is cared for by the Aubrey Fletcher family who have restored the Church of St Mary, a building full of interesting detail and monuments. Notable is the Gate House, dated 1680, with its Restoration windows. It was once used as a laundry for the big house. There are superb views on all roads.

The Claydons, Middle, East, Botolph, and Steeple, should all be visited in conjunction with Claydon House, home of the Verney family. The whole area has a remote and peaceful atmosphere and the landscaping of a great park. The Verney papers tell a wealth of stories about these villages which seem little changed since the days when highwaymen abounded, or people arrived with stories of the great fire of London, or the news of Waterloo. In East Claydon Sir Arthur Bryant once lived in White Lodge, a favourite home. The village has a small, stone, square-towered church, with ancient carving and a chime of five bells. There is an unusual thatched bus-shelter built around an oak tree.

Creslow. Manor House, now a farm, is thought to be the oldest inhabited dwelling in Buckinghamshire. It was built of stone about 1330 but was much altered in the seventeenth and eighteenth centuries. It has a magnificent crypt, groined roof and carved bosses. The remains of the church were once used as a dovecote. In Tudor times the enormous pastures supplied beef for the royal table, and cattle still graze there. Westcar, a farmer in the eighteenth century, first sent cattle from these pastures by canal to London (*cf* Whitchurch).

***Cublington** will never be forgotten as the centre of the greatest fight for the environment that has ever been waged. The solidarity of the villagers, supported by their neighbours and most of England, fought the Government's decision to obliterate them by placing the third London Airport at Wing. It has now returned to its peaceful, isolated life. Approached by gated roads with fine sweeping views, the village offers the Church, the Manor, Old Rectory, Neals Farm and the Beacon (Mount of an old Roman Castle) as buildings of interest.

In 1972 four hundred trees were planted at a crossroads in the centre of the proposed site, and the great battle for the environment commemorated on a monument designed by Neil Morton. The inscription reads:

CUBLINGTON SPINNEY
This spinney was planted in 1972
by the Buckinghamshire County Council
in gratitude to all those who supported
the campaign against the recommendation
that London's Third Airport should be at Cublington.
Parish councils, organisations, societies
and many individuals
contributed towards the costs of the Spinney.
This point is the centre
of the area proposed for the Airport.

Mid-most unmitigated England

Cuddington, derivation 'Cudda's Farm', contains 'Spurt Street' (1320, la sperte, i.e. spirit, a jet of liquid) where several springs remain. For centuries much of the land belonged to the Dean and Chapter of Rochester. Holyman's Farm commemorates a family from which sprang the Bishop of Bristol who opposed the divorce of Queen Katharine and Henry VIII. The church tower is a landmark for miles. There are many delightful old cottages; Tyringham Hall is mainly seventeenth century but with the king post of an earlier house. Until recently it belonged to the family of Nether Winchendon.

Dinton should be approached from the low road, the Portway, not from the A418, in order to get the full benefit of the cluster of church and village among chestnut trees. The church, well kept, has over the south door a splendid tympanum of Christ in Glory, and below can be seen Jonah partly in the whale's mouth. South of the churchyard are the old stocks. The Elizabethan manor house, with zig-zag striped tiles, was once the home of Simon Mayne, one of the Regicides. His servant, the Dinton hermit, is alleged to have been Charles I's executioner. Later the Hall belonged to the Van Hattems; the first of this family came to England as an admiral with William III. Sir John Van Hattem built the 'Castle' or folly to house his collection of fossils. The Glebe House is the largest witchert house in Buckinghamshire. The hamlets of Westlington and Upton on the West and East of Dinton are almost a continuation of the village. Both contain pretty cottages, and fortunately the modern additions to Westlington have not been allowed to intrude.

Doddershall. Since 1490 the descendants of Sergeant Pigott have lived in Doddershall Park. The fine house forms three sides of a square; the north wing is Tudor, the centre is Elizabethan, while joined to the south wing is a Jacobean Hall built in 1688. The village is a hamlet of Quainton. A dip into the history of the Pigott family makes worthwhile reading – to wit *Papers from an Iron Chest* by G. Eland.

Dorton is now well known for Ashfold preparatory school which occupies the fine Jacobean mansion with its seventeenth-century front and interior decorations, including especially fine Jacobean ceilings. A small chapel restored by Sir Henry Aubrey Fletcher is used by the school. The boys are delegated to show visitors round and an artistic and informative booklet on the house is available. A mineral spring here once raised hopes of turning Dorton into a spa (*cf* Brill).

Drayton Beauchamp. The church has some interesting brasses and is lovingly kept in fine shape by the present rector. At one time it was the custom for the rector to supply the villagers with as much bread, cheese and ale as they wanted on St Stephen's day. One year a 'penurious old bachelor' rector refused to be so generous and barred himself in the rectory, but the villagers stormed the house from the roof, helping themselves to whatever they could find. The parishioners kept up this 'stephening' for as long as they could, but it was discontinued in 1827 – funds ran out.

***Dunton** is a tiny village in quiet farmland. The church is simple and unrestored. Note the vicarage. There is also a finely restored farmhouse. The Rev. Sillitoe was a militant resister during the anti-airport fight.

Edgcott. The Church of St Michael stands high among well-kept buildings and cottages, commanding long views. There is a sundial on the tower. Lawn House is Tudor and has a double staircase.

Ellesborough. If you plan to explore the hills on foot this is the ideal point at which to start. The village lies on the upper Icknield Way just where it crosses the lower slopes of the hills. Coombe Hill (National Trust), the highest point of the Chilterns, lies in this parish; also Beacon Hill, which rises directly from the road. Visitors are asked to keep to the footpaths and not to trespass on the Chequers estate. The path emerges finally at Cadsdean, just above Monks Risborough, after leading through woods. The Perpendicular church stands on the top of a small spur visible for miles. Successive Prime Ministers have read the Lessons here and have also played golf on Ellesborough golf course.

Eythrope. In 1490 Sir Roger Dynham founded a chapel here where he hoped eventually to be buried. At one period it belonged to the Dormers. Early in the eighteenth century Eythrope belonged to Sir William Stanhope, one of the 'monks' of Medmenham. He added to the chapel and celebrated divine service there regularly for ten years, yet in 1738 he most wickedly pulled it down and used its stones to build a bridge over the Thame. This family, which was the Chesterfield line, also had a big house, Denham, near Quainton, which suffered the same fate. The story goes that the sixth Earl of Chesterfield destroyed Eythrope in a fury because he was not made Lord Lieutenant of the County. The catalogue of the demolition sale remains.

Fleet Marston. Marston means 'marshy ground', which is appropriate for this hamlet. The small church stands alone in the fields, and is without a tower. It dates from the twelfth and thirteenth centuries and has a fine queen-post roof in the nave. In ancient times Fleet Marston was important by virtue of its situation at the junction of a Roman and medieval by-road from Dorchester with Akeman Street, the road to Bath.

Ford. This hamlet, sitting among low-lying water meadows, is actually in Dinton parish. The Dinton Hermit Inn is named after the supposed executioner of Charles I, who lived in a cave near the Folly.

Gibraltar recalls the legend of eighty refugees from the Great Plague in London, 1665, who walked here to take shelter with a relative of one of their group. The day after arrival a child sickened with the plague and forty deaths followed rapidly, all victims being buried in a mass grave.

Grandborough. This is a remote little village set among large pastures. The small church has a surprise – a fifteenth-century christmatory or pewter box, now among the church plate, was found built into the wall. This was used for administering holy oil with tow; when found the tow was still oily.

Grendon Underwood. St Leonard's Church seems remarkably tall. There is a marble effigy of John Piggott of Doddershall. From the sixteenth century the village was a stopping place on the road between Warwickshire and London. The rough handling that Shakespeare received from two constables when he stayed at the then Ship Inn is supposed to have suggested the humour of *A Midsummer Night's Dream*. 'Shakespeare House' recalls the tradition. The open prison has modernised the whole aspect and atmosphere of the village.

Great and Little Kimble. The name is said to be derived from Cymbeline, a British king who lived at the beginning of the Christian era; it is probably the oldest village name in Buckinghamshire. Great Kimble is built on the Upper Icknield Way. It was in the church here that John Hampden, on 9th January 1635, made his protest against the imposition of Ship Money by Charles I. A facsimile of the demand for Ship Money is on the wall. His trial was one of the first events which led to the Civil War.

Little Kimble is on the edge of the Chequers estate, with Ragpit Hill,

Pulpit Hill and the Cymbeline's Mount behind. The undistinguished Church of All Saints, with its small bellcote, contains some of the most artistic fourteenth-century wall-paintings in Buckinghamshire. Note especially St George and St Francis preaching to the birds, of which there is only one other representation in England.

Haddenham. 'Haeda's Homestead' should be explored on foot. Notice the houses and walls made largely of witchert. This material is typical of Buckinghamshire, as are the walls which were often thatched or tiled to charming effect. Church Green has a duck pond and attractive, well-preserved houses. Flint Street is the oldest street. Fort End Square, Town End Green and Skittles Green give the feeling of several villages joined together. The houses are connected by narrow, walled alleys, called 'tails', which fortunately were not burnt down in the large fires which occurred in 1701 and 1760. A local 'jibe' says 'At Haddenham folks put their foot out of the window to see if it's time to get up'.

During World War II the Duke of Richmond and Gordon started a factory for making airscrews, which has since developed into Airtech, employing local people. H.M. Queen Elizabeth The Queen Mother, then the Queen of George VI, visited here and had tea at the Old Vicarage where the Duke was living. The ferry pilots, many of them girls in the WAAF, used to land planes on the airfield, which was also used during the war for 'underground' missions to the Continent. The Playing Field was opened by H.R.H. Prince Philip on 4th October 1959.

Hardwick. Some villages appear to have 'just grown' but this is a well-constructed place on a slight rise not far from the main road. The church has several interesting features – a tablet on a tomb outside the south wall commemorates the mass burial of eighty Cavaliers who fell in the Battle of Aylesbury, 1643. The remains were found during road excavations at a bridge north of Aylesbury, and removed to Hardwick.

Hartwell. At the geological junction of the Portland Sands with the Hartwell clay, Hartwell is noted for its springs. One of them has an Egyptian-style building erected over it by Dr John Lee who lived at Hartwell House. Traditionally, it was the spring where harts quenched their thirst, this giving Hartwell its name.

> Stay traveller! Round thy horse's neck the bridle fling,
> and taste the water of the Hartwell Spring;
> Then say which offers thee the better cheer –
> The Hartwell water or the Aylesbury beer!

The fame of the house lies in the fact that King Louis XVIII of France and his Court spent years of exile under its roof; as a courtesy one of the roads out of Aylesbury is called 'Bourbon Street'.

The local clay used for bricks contains many rare fossils. Note the park wall. The bridge in the park is the central arch of old Kew Bridge rebuilt here.

Lower Hartwell has a feudal atmosphere. The rectory is built on the site of a fifteenth-century house; the red-brick Bailiff's House is also of interest. Hartwell House, long connected with the Lee family, is now the House of Citizenship. It is a fine Jacobean mansion with a superb staircase, restored after a recent fire and visited by H.M. Queen Elizabeth, The Queen Mother, on 29th June 1965. The village's busiest time was probably that of its occupation by members of the exiled Court of France.

Hoggeston. A small, compact, once stockaded, village well worth a visit. The settlement was protected by banks of earth, which also embraced two ponds; cattle were driven into the stockades at night. The church should be carefully examined – do not overlook the recumbent figure of William de Birmingham, owner of the manor, who holds the model of a building which he founded. His feet rest on a dog, showing that he died in his bed. In those days churches often had hassocks of 'tossock', a thick slab of peaty soil covered with dried grass, of which there is an example in the church.

Hogshaw means Hog Wood. Connected with Knights Hospitallers, it is a small hamlet of farmhouses with sixteenth-century and later relics and remains, some of which came from the former church.

Horsenden. In the seventeenth century it was on the main road between London and Oxford. The church, as well as the Manor House, was then enclosed by a moat. Browne Willis states that the house was garrisoned by Sir John Denham for King Charles I, though it was surrounded by Parliamentary strongholds at Wycombe, Chinnor, Thame, Hampden, Aylesbury and Dinton. In 1820, and 1900, iron cannon balls and stone catapult balls (*petrariae*) were found in the moat. A chest full of weapons of the Civil War period was found on the rafters under the roof. Of the church, dedicated to St Michael and All Angels, little more than the fifteenth-century chancel remains. There is a sixteenth-century rood screen at the west end of the present nave.

Hulcott. If you like village greens you will find a fine example here including an old church (its weathered bell-turret on strong, internally visible, timbers) and cottages clustered among lime trees. It is a village secluded from the roar of modern life, just off the main road.

Ickford. On the sill of the east window in the north aisle of the church is a rough marking of the game called Nine Men's Morris. Relics of this pastime are now rare, but at the height of its popularity it could often be found marked out on village greens, cathedral benches and church porches. The risk of flooding by the River Thame of the surrounding water meadows limits modern building. You will find fords and raised planked footways – the so-called 'Postman's Walk'.

Ilmer. A small village down a tree-shaded cul-de-sac in flat country near the Oxfordshire border. The Manor of Ilmer was, at the end of the eleventh century, held by a sub-feudatory of the powerful Bishop of Bayeux for the service of keeping the King's Hawks, a contract which continued for several centuries. There is a pointed steeple on the little church beside the small rectory. Shell-Mex experimental farms and a nursery garden keep the village up to date.

Kingsey (King's Island). Well-set in its surroundings of water meadows stretching to Scotsgrove mill, which has been worked from 1395 until recently, it lies close to the Thame. The termination 'ey' reveals that there were originally little islands in this marshy area. The church was rebuilt in the Gothic manner in 1892–93. The village is dominated by Tythrop House, long the home of the Wykehams, now occupied by Mr and Mrs Jeremy Cotton, who have carefully removed Victorian and other accretions and restored the original brick façade and Carolean hipped roof. It has a beautifully carved staircase reputed to be by Grinling Gibbons or one of his followers.

Kingswood in 1298 was called The Lord King's Wood. As its name suggests the kings hunted in the old Bernwood forest which once covered these fields. It is associated with Fair Rosamund. 'Rosiman's Waye' is shown on Lipscombe's map.

Long Crendon. A tour of this pleasant village should begin at the church; it is worth buying the booklet to learn about it. The Court House next door is fifteenth-century, a National Trust property, open to the public. There is also an old manor house given by William the Conqueror to Walter Giffard. In the thirteenth century the manor was divided into three parts and owned by the Deans and Canons of St George's, Windsor; All Soul's College, Oxford; and the Dormer family. The High Street is full of cottages and houses of varied styles, all restored. Long Crendon was chosen in Coronation year, 1952, as the typical English village, filmed extensively in colour, and shown all over the world. From 1600 to 1862 this village had a prosperous needlemaking industry. Many of the women also made lace. Later in the nineteenth century the cottagers were famous for fattening the well-known Aylesbury ducklings.

Long Marston is regarded as one of the outskirt villages of the Vale. A witch-ducking is alleged to have taken place in the village pond – now the site of the War Memorial – the last witch-trial having been recorded in 1751.

Longwick. 'Wic' means dairy farm. It is a long straggling village with several farms and many new houses. Good food and drink can be had at the Red Lion.

Ludgershall. The houses are set wide apart and this gives the village an extraordinarily remote feeling. One can imagine the Romans marching down Akeman Street, their road between Aylesbury and Bicester. There is an unusual font in the church, but one of the most intriguing sights is the sculpture of happy faces, obviously of local characters, whose cowled heads and intertwined arms, make capitals to the pillars; also note the oak carving on the roof. The living was once held by John Wycliffe.

Marsh was probably once, according to its name, undrained swampy land, but is now a pleasant scatter of houses and a lonely inn giving fine views of the Chilterns. Birds soar undisturbed from these sheltered fields. The fritillary, or snake lily, grows wild in marshy fields such as these.

Marsh Gibbon. The Elizabethan and Jacobean manor house was built *circa* 1560. St Mary's Church is mostly thirteenth century; note the coffin lid of that era with its elaborately foliated cross. The village is rich in notable buildings, some thirty-six being listed under preservation orders.

Meadle. An old Quaker Meeting House was situated here; now there are isolated farms dotted round the low-lying meadows.

Mentmore could well be named as the starting point of the Vale. Set in a park, at the end of a double avenue of chestnuts, the great mansion looks like a turreted mirage floating over the trees. It was built in 1852–54 by Sir Joseph Paxton and his son-in-law, G. H. Stokes, for Baron Amschel de Rothschild (whose daughter married Lord Rosebery).

Monks Risborough belonged to Christchurch, Canterbury, before the Norman conquest. St Dunstan's Church, externally restored by Street, suggests the fourteenth century in its internal details. The Dovecot, Whiteleaf Cross on the hill, and the Mound, a neolithic barrow, are all of interest.

Nether Winchendon. The ochre colour-wash on the old cottages was made from earth dug at Wheatley. The unspoilt Church of St Nicholas is mainly fourteenth-century, and contains box pews, a three-decker pulpit and small stained glass of the fifteenth and sixteenth centuries, also fifteenth-century brasses. The early eighteenth-century clock was restored in 1968. The church is appropriately dedicated to the patron saint of fishermen, for the Thame once yielded fine fish. Now the fishing rights are let for the benefit of the church to Airtech angling club. On May-Day, following an ancient tradition, the children carry a flower-decorated shrine and garlands from house to house, singing a song. Most of the houses and cottages are timber-framed; when in World War II two land mines fell in the village, the old timbers stood the strain better than the houses of brick or stone.

Nether Winchendon House is medieval with early Tudor additions and eighteenth-century details. In the Tudor parlour there is a fine Early Renaissance frieze in carved oak. The house was once the home of Sir Francis Bernard, last English Governor of Massachusetts Bay. Bernardston and Winchendon, Massachusetts, and Bernardsville, New Jersey, were all named after him. His descendants are still living in the house.

North Marston. The Church of St Mary was restored in 1855 at the expense of Queen Victoria in memory of J. C. Nield who had left her £250,000 in his will. She chose Sir Matthew Digby Wyatt to carry out the highly ornate work. The local spring, blessed by John Schorne, rector from 1290, was used by physicians of Aylesbury and Winslow in making up medicines for eye diseases, gout and rheumatism. John Schorne was reputed to have conjured the devil into a boot, a place where he could do no harm, hence the origin of the Jack-in-a-Box. The many 'Boot' inns in Buckinghamshire commemorate this incident in their signs.

Oakley lies in the water meadows. Several of the pleasant seventeenth-century farms and cottages are built of Flemish brick. The Great Train Robbers chose a remote farm here for their hide-out on 8th August 1963, when they absconded with over £2,500,000.

Over Winchendon. Over Winchendon House once served as the kitchen and offices of the Marquess of Wharton's fine mansion. As it is stone under brick facing it is believed to be the surviving part of an earlier medieval house. A summer-house, somewhat in Vanbrugh's style, remains from the Wharton gardens. The property passed through the hands of the Marlborough Trustees to Baron Ferdinand de Rothschild (*cf* Waddesdon). The Church of St Mary Magdalene, mainly Norman, has a brass of Sir John Studeley, vicar, who died in 1502. The pulpit is probably fourteenth-century. Note the funeral helmet.

Oving. The name derives from 'Ufa's people'. All Saints' Church was much restored by Street in 1867. The Chancel is early thirteenth-century; the rood screen is Perpendicular. Oving House was built early in the seventeenth century and has fine baroque interiors. The main street has wide green verges and pretty cottages; one of the original pumps still stands in a recess in Church Road. An old cottage on the outskirts is known as 'the pest house'; while Bunhill ('Bone Hill') presumably records the place where bodies were thrown during a severe outbreak of plague. The most memorable feature, however, is the wide panorama of the Vale as seen from the ridge bordering the village.

Owlswick offers the Shoulder of Mutton inn, and nearby Waldridge Manor where Cromwell is reputed to have stabled his horses before the Battle of Postcombe. The oak-mullioned and diamond-paned windows and immense chimney stacks are noteworthy. The cartoonist of World War I, Bruce Bairnsfather, lived here for some time.

Piddington, Oxon, has an historic churchyard; the appropriately simple inscriptions on the old tombstones are worth reading. Ralph the Hermit lived at nearby St Cross Chapel, Muswell Hill, in 1102. The clergy moved to St Nicholas's Church in 1428. Note the early font, alms box, and wall painting of St Christopher. The saint's picture was usually seen opposite the door, so that travellers could quickly look into the church and offer a short prayer to their patron.

Pitchcott, like many other villages in the Vale, stands at the highest point of its area. Its buildings have become landmarks to visitors, particularly as their white stone makes them conspicuous.

Princes Risborough. *Hrisebyrgan be Chilternes etese* 1006, means 'Brushwood by Chiltern eaves'. To the south-west of the church lay the castle of the Black Prince, so-called because he wore black armour. Fragments of a rampart, a ditch, and walls have been found. The Black Prince is said to have had a stud here. The Church of St Mary is built of flint, with a graceful steeple. In the Manor House opposite, now a property of the National Trust, many pictures from the National Gallery in London were stored for safety during the bombing of World War II. The old vicarage is a picturesque timber-framed cottage of the fifteenth century. The Town Hall in the market square, built in 1824, is used still for the market below, the meeting house above.

Quainton. The careful brickwork of a tower windmill dominates the informal village green, with its seventeenth-century houses. The local historian, Dr George Lipscomb, was born in the village. Note the splendid Winwood alms houses, 1687. The church, c.1360, is rich in brasses and Renaissance sculpture by Grinling Gibbons, Giacomo Leoni and Rysbrack. Nearby is Denham Lodge, a completely moated farmhouse; brick walls, extending a considerable distance from the Lodge, are the remains of a deer park.

Quarrendon (Mill Hill). Sir Henry Lee entertained Queen Elizabeth I here in 1592, but now nothing remains of the mansion of the Lee family, once one of the most notable in Buckinghamshire, except the ruins in the field of St Peter's Church. The Lees were connected by marriage to many families in the Vale and once owned Hartwell and Chequers. The last member of the family presented Chequers to the nation as a country retreat for Prime Ministers. (See *Related to Lee* by Colonel R. Melville Lee, nephew of Lord Lee of Fareham.)

Rowsham has a bridge over the Thame, and a few farm houses. The finely-worked 'laid' hedges of this area were photographed by *The Times* as an example of an old country craft.

Sedrup. A small grouping, near the Bugle Horn inn, of modern 'executive-type' detached houses of the '60s set in open gardens. It is attached to the parish of Stone.

Shabbington rises above low water meadows, necessitating many foot-bridges, and has a mixture of small houses set at different angles and constructed of different materials which seem to assert the individuality and independence of each age.

***Soulbury** has an interesting large stone in the middle of the road, close by Lovett's Grammar School. It is a 'glacial erratic' left behind at the end of the Glacial epoch, said to be a species of Derbyshire Millstone Grit, which the ice carried well over a hundred miles. A local superstition says the stone has magical powers and that it rolled to Soulbury on its own.

***Stewkley,** said to be one of the longest villages in England, has two miles of continuous street stretching along a ridge. The houses are a typically English mixture of sizes, styles and periods. The Norman Church is internationally famous as one of the most splendid examples of its period and played a vital part in the defence of this area from the Third London Airport.

Stoke Hammond. Note Tyrrell's Manor farmhouse, two-storey eighteenth-century brick, well-proportioned, with its stone quoins. St Luke's Church is of ironstone with a central tower, fourteenth-century font, alms box dated

1618, a monument to the Disney family, c.1690, and other interesting details. The three locks and several hump bridges over the canal give the landscape a unique quality.

Stoke Mandeville, named for its connection with the de Mandeville family, is now renowned throughout the world for its hospital for paraplegics. Her Majesty the Queen opened the unique Sports Stadium connected with this hospital on 2nd August 1969. There are still occasional thatched and timber cottages within the village, and old inns among the modern development. John Hampden owned land here and from here also he defied King Charles I regarding the assessment for Ship Money. A monument now stands on the actual spot at Prestwood. It was at a parish meeting that Ship Money was demanded by assessors Aldridge and Lane and constables Goodchild and Rutland, names still to be found in the district. (*cf* Great Kimble).

Stone. The name comes from Old English (Saxon) 'Stan' and was the meeting place, marked by a conspicuous stone, of the Aylesbury Hundred. Approaching from the south one gets a view of the church and its surrounding rose-brick buildings. Roman pottery has been found here, and a Roman villa stood where Alwyn Lawn is today. Before the Conquest all the land belonged to Alwyn the Saxon; after the Conquest it was given to Peverell the Norman, and the Court still bears his name.

For those interested in brass rubbing, the twelfth-century Church of St John the Baptist contains good studies of William Gurney and his wife, 1472, and Thomas Gurney and his wife, 1520. There is a superb font which originally came from Hampstead Norris.

The modern development of Stone is dominated by St John's Hospital and its complex of buildings and nurses' homes, all with extensive views. The hospital was visited by H.R.H. the Duchess of Kent (Princess Marina) on 20th June 1959. Part of the hospital was designed in the 1850s by T. H. Wyatt and D. Brandon.

Swanbourne, on the borders of the Vale, is widely known for its preparatory school. It has a group of good houses, particularly the Elizabethan manor and Deverell's Farm, 1632, with its mullioned windows. St Swithin's Church, much of which is early thirteenth-century, has faintly discernible wall-paintings of *c*.1500.

Terrick House, built in 1702, has a pleasant façade with cross windows, said to have been built in thanks that the Great Plague passed by the house (*cf* Gate House, Chilton). A group of small houses stands on the Lower Icknield Way.

Thame. Though just over the county boundary, Thame marks the south-west limit of the Vale. It is a perfect example of a market town, with its wide main street, variety of shops, and an open-air market on Tuesdays. Its many inns – the Bird Cage, Spread Eagle, Swan, Fighting Cocks, Eight Bells, to name only a few – have changed little since the days when Thame was one of the main coaching towns between London and Oxford. The Bullingdon

House in the Buttermarket has a vine on which grapes ripen. All the inns have painted signs. The church and the old Grammar School are interesting buildings to visit.

Many small industries make Thame a lively and busy place, but it is most widely known for its one-day agricultural show, said to be the largest in southern England, and for the traditional Fair, which is held in the main street and lasts for three days.

Upton is a hamlet with farm cottages and several fine stone houses. Now enlarged by a variety of modern bungalows it still has splendid views towards the Chilterns (*cf* Dinton).

Waddesdon is a Rothschild village developed at the turn of the century. The magnificent 2,000-acre grounds of Waddesdon Manor, include a deer park, and the treasure-filled house. They are open to the public during the summer as a property of the National Trust, the gift of the late James de Rothschild. The newly restored aviary, set in a rose garden near the house, is also of particular interest and contains a variety of parrots, cockatoos and tropical birds. In the village church there is a brass dated 1490.

Weedon village has had a preservation order placed on it by the Buckinghamshire County Council to prevent the overspill from Aylesbury from spoiling its character. The modern in-filling has been carefully concealed among the variety of well-preserved houses and cottages which include Manor Farm, dated 1649. The entrance gateway, 1687, and the barn, 1647, are also marked. There is a pleasant inn, the Wheatsheaf. Bones of prehistoric creatures have been found in the Kimmeridge clay of this area.

Westlington has a medley of cottages, mostly thatched, around the green, with which harmonise two well-designed modern houses of the same colour and pitch of roof. Note the brick and flint barn beside the White Horse inn, once also thatched (*cf* Dinton).

Weston Turville. The village was called Weston in 1004; after the Norman Conquest Turville was added, named for one of William the Conqueror's companions in arms. The de Turville family is last mentioned in the records in 1300. In the Church of St Mary the Virgin the most priceless possession is the fifteenth-century glass in the east window. Note the stone sarcophagus, 1050, the Aylesbury font, 1160, and the brass, 1580, depicting a citizen in a fur robe. The peal of five bells dates from 1460. There is a swing gate with a huge weight. The rose-brick Georgian manor house is of two different styles; the flint and brick rectory, 1838, by Sir Giles Gilbert Scott. Many fine small village houses can be seen among the modern development of the last thirty years.

*****Whitchurch** is a large village on the main road between Aylesbury and Buckingham. A Norman castle of the de Bolebecs was demolished in the Civil War, 1642–46, the site is marked by the moat, bailey and the spring called 'Fair Alice'. The Court House, built in 1360, is now a hotel; many other fine houses in the village date from the sixteenth and seventeenth centuries. The Church of St John the Evangelist, partly thirteenth-century, was built on the site of a Saxon church, and a wonderful view of the Vale can be seen from its tower. Queen Elizabeth I merged Creslow (*q.v.*) with Whitchurch. This church now contains a Creslow Manor box-pew and a monument to John Westcar. Rex Whistler's family lived for a time in Whitchurch, in Bolebec House; his painting of the Vale is the view from that garden.

Whiteleaf Cross on the Chiltern escarpment is the western boundary of the Vale and a local landmark. It is one of the officially listed ancient monuments. Its origins are uncertain, but a charter of A.D. 903 refers to a boundary mark that may have been this cross in an earlier form. The most likely theory is that it was the work of nearby monks at Monks Risborough or Missenden Abbey. Scouring and cleaning the cross is still a festive occasion for local residents. Lipscomb, 1837, mentions the custom: 'It is now borne by the neighbourhood and never without a merrymaking'.

***Wing**, one of the larger villages, was the centre of local resistance to the siting of the Third London Airport. The Anglo-Saxon Church of All Saints is one of the finest in England, and is unusually large for its period. There is a Perpendicular font and Jacobean pulpit. The Dormer monuments are superb.

Wingrave. As in all these villages the interest here lies in the long continuous historic association with the church, and the fact that it is still a living entity.

Wotton Underwood, pronounced 'Wooton', is adjacent to Bernwood forest. Wotton House with its two service pavilions dominates the quiet village of farms and parsonage which lie close to the church. The 'Bunch' and the 'Row', once contiguous cottages, have been cleverly restored. All Saints' Church is full of interest; it contains memorials and armorial glass of the Grenville family. The parish owns Elizabethan communion plate, dated the year after the Armada, and a Breeches Bible.

Select Bibliography
AND LIST FOR FURTHER READING

Bates, H. E., *The Face of England*; B. T. Batsford Ltd, 1939.
Bateson, F. W., *Brill: A Short History*; Brill Society Publications, 1966.
Bergamar, Kate, *The Bucks Explorer*; Shire Publications, 1968.
Betjeman, John, and John Piper, *Buckinghamshire Architectural Guide*; John Murray Ltd, 1948.
Brewer, J. Norris, *Introduction to the Beauties of England & Wales*; 1818.
Brooke, Rupert, *The Collected Poems of Rupert Brooke*; Sidgwick & Jackson Ltd, 1918.
Bryant, Sir Arthur, *Extract from Evidence set before the Roskill Commission*; H.M.S.O., 1970.
Bryant, Sir Arthur, *The Lion and the Unicorn*; William Collins, Sons & Co., Ltd, 1969.
Buchanan, Sir Colin, Extract from the *Note of Dissent*, 18th December 1970; H.M.S.O.
Camden, William, *Britannia*; 1607.
Camp, John, *Oxfordshire and Buckinghamshire Pubs*; B. T. Batsford Ltd, 1965.
Chambers, E. K., *Sir Henry Lee, an Elizabethan Portrait*; Clarendon Press, Oxford, 1936.
Clear, A., *1000 Years of Winslow Life*; Edwin French, Winslow, 1894.
Clear, A., *A Bucks Worthy, Benjamin Keach*; Edwin French, Winslow, 1908.
Cobbett, William, *Cobbett's Rural Rides*, 1829; J. M. Dent & Sons Ltd.
Cooper, C. D., *Long Crendon, England's Coronation Village*; F. H. Castle & Co. Ltd, 1953.
Defoe, Daniel, *A Tour through England & Wales, 1724–1726*; Everyman's Library.
Dodd, Rev. W., *Thoughts in Prison*; 1781.
Donald, Joyce, *A Short History of Long Crendon*; 1971.
Drayton, Michael, *Polyolbion*; 1612.
Druce, George C., *The Flora of Buckinghamshire*; T. Buncle & Co., 1926.
Eland, G. (ed.), *Papers from an Iron Chest at Doddershall*; G. T. de Fraine & Co. Ltd, 1937.
Eland, G., *Old Works and Past Days in Rural Buckinghamshire*; G. T. de Fraine & Co. Ltd, 1921.
Eland, G., *The Chilterns and the Vale*; Longmans, Green & Co. Ltd, 1911.
Eriksen, Svend, *Waddesdon Manor, a Guide to the House*: The National Trust, 1965.

Fowler, J. F. K., *Records of Old Times*; 1898.
Fowler, J. F. K., *Echoes of Old County Life*; 1892.
Freemantle, Anne, *The Wynne Diaries, Vol. III*; Oxford University Press, 1935–1940.
Gerard's *Herbal*; 1597.
Gibbs, Robert, *Bucks Miscellany*; 1891.
Gibbs, Robert, *A History of Aylesbury*; 1885, Paul P. B. Minet (reprinted 1971).
Gomme, G. L., *The Village Community*; 1890.
Gomme, G. L., *The Gentleman's Magazine Library*, 1731–1868.
Grenville, G. N., *Legends of the Library at Lilies*; 1832, Longmans, Green & Co. Ltd.
Grigson, Geoffrey, *A Herbal of All Sorts*; 1959.
Harman, H., *Buckinghamshire Dialect*; S.R. Publications 1929 (reprinted 1970).
Harman, H., *Sketches of the Bucks Countryside*; Blandford Press Ltd, 1934.
Head, J. F., *Early Man in South Buckinghamshire*; John Wright & Sons Ltd, 1955.
Higgins, *The Bernards of Abington and Nether Winchendon*; Longmans, Green & Co. Ltd, 1903.
Holloway, Joseph, *Two Lectures on the History of Whitchurch*; 1889.
Howard, H. Evelyn, *Landmarks*; edited by Hamilton & Arlott, Cambridge University Press, 1943.
James, William, and Jacob Malcolm, *A General View of Agriculture in Bucks*; 1794.
Kennedy, Alexander W. M., *The Birds of Berkshire & Buckinghamshire*; Ingleton & Drake Ltd, 1868.
Lamb, Cadbury, *Discovering Buckinghamshire*; (pamphlet) 1967.
Leland, J., *The Itinerary of John Leland*, 1540; Centaur Press Ltd, 1964.
Lipscomb, Dr George, *The History and Antiquities of the County of Buckingham*; J. & W. Robins, 1847.
Lovett Family, *The Lovetts of Bucks, 1066–1912*; edited 1912.
Lowndes, C., *Dinton Hall and Church*; G. T. de Fraine & Co. Ltd, 1872.
Lowndes, C., *Lecture on the History of Hartwell and Stone*; James Pickburn, 1862.
Macdonell, A. G., *England, Their England*; Macmillan and Co. Ltd., 1959.
Massingham, H. J., *This Plot of Earth*; William Collins, Sons & Co. Ltd, 1944.
Mawer, A., and F. M. Stenton, *The Placenames of Buckinghamshire*; 1925.
Morton, Frederick, *The Rothschilds*; Secker & Warburg, 1962.
Nash, John, *The Shell Guide to Buckinghamshire*; B. T. Batsford Ltd, 1936.
National Trust Booklet, *Claydon House, Buckinghamshire*.
Page, William (ed.), *The Victoria History of the County of Buckingham*; St Catherine's Press, 1925.

Parker, T. J., *Quainton 50 Years Ago*; G. T. de Fraine & Co. Ltd, 1915.
Pevsner, Nikolaus, *The Buildings of England*; Penguin Books, 1960.
Pitkin, Thomas, *A Bucks Labourer*; (pamphlet), Winslow Printers, 1894.
Rose, Walter, *Fifty Years Ago*; 1920.
Rose, Walter, *Good Neighbours*; 1942.
Royal Commission on Historical Monuments in Buckinghamshire, Vol. II; H.M.S.O., 1913.
Salter, H. E., *The Boarstall Cartulary*; Clarendon Press, Oxford, 1930.
Sheahan, J. J., *History & Topography of Buckinghamshire*; Longmans, Green & Co. Ltd, 1862.
Shiner, L. M., *800 Years; Being a Tale of Stewkley 1150–1950*; (pamphlet), 1950.
Shrimpton, W., *Notes on a Decayed Needleland*; (pamphlet), reprinted from the *Redditch Indicator*, 1897.
Underwood, Peter, *Gazetteer of British Ghosts*; Souvenir Press Ltd, 1971.
Uttley, Alison, *Buckinghamshire*; Robert Hale & Co., 1950.
Verney, Frances Parthenope, *Memoirs of the Verney Family during the Civil War, Vol. II*, 1892; reprinted by the Woburn Press, London, 1970.
Verney, Margaret M., *Bucks Biographies*; Clarendon Press, Oxford, 1912.
Verney, Sir Harry, *The Verneys of Claydon*; Pergamon Press, 1968.
Ward, F. J., *The Church of Kimble Magna in John Hampden's Time*; (pamphlet).
Whistler, Laurence, *The World's Room*, Collected Poems; William Heinemann, 1949.
Wright, Doreen, *Bobbin Lace Making*; G. Bell & Sons Ltd, 1971.
Wright, Thomas, *The Romance of the Lace Pillow*; H. H. Armstrong, 1925–1930.

Acknowledgements

A collection such as this is made possible only by permission of the authors and publishers who hold the copyrights. To all who have granted such permission we extend our thanks, as follows:

To the Woburn Press, London, for permission to reprint excerpts from *The Memoirs of the Verney Family*, by Frances Parthenope Verney; to the Ariel Press, Ltd, for permission to reprint F. C. Turner's paintings of the Vale of Aylesbury Steeplechase; to Sir John Betjeman, C.B.E., for his permission to reprint extracts from his evidence given before the Roskill Commission; also to quote from his letter to the *Friends* regarding Thomas Scott; to the Blandford Press Ltd, for permission to quote from *Sketches of the Bucks Countryside*, by H. Harman; to the Centaur Press Ltd, for permission to reprint extracts from *The Itinerary of John Leland*, by John Leland; to the Clarendon Press, Oxford, for permission to print the passages on St Osyth, Benjamin Keach and John Schorne, from *Bucks Biographies*, by Margaret M. Verney; to J. M. Dent and Sons, Ltd, for permission to print the extracts from Cobbett's *Rural Rides* and Defoe's *Tour Through England and Wales*, Everyman's Library; to Robert Hale and Company, for permission to quote from *Buckinghamshire*, by Alison Uttley; to Her Majesty's Stationery Office, for permission to reprint extracts from the Report of the Roskill Commission on the Third London Airport; to Macmillan and Company Ltd, for permission to use the extract from *England, Their England*, by A. G. Macdonell; to Paul P. B. Minet, for permission to quote from *A History of Aylesbury*, by Robert Gibbs; to Ian Rodger, for permission to quote from his article 'Megalithic Mathematics' which appeared in *The Listener*, 27th November 1969; to Sidgwick and Jackson Ltd, for permission to reprint 'The Chilterns', from *The Collected Poems of Rupert Brooke*; to The Society of Authors, for permission to print the extract from *This Plot of Earth*, by H. J. Massingham.

To *Bucks Life and Thames Valley Countryside*, for permission to quote the following articles which appeared in their magazine: 'Florence Nightingale, 1820–1910', by Sir Harry Verney; 'Three Men of Dinton', by Eric Rayner; 'Lacemaking in Buckinghamshire', by Anne Craig Howie; 'Great Hampden and the Patriot', by Anne James; 'A Victorian Sensation', by Anne Craig Howie; 'Powerhouses of the Past', by J. N. T. Vince; 'The Witchert Villages of West Bucks', by Norman Good.

To A. D. Peters and Company, Ltd, for permission to reprint an extract from *The Rothschilds*, by Frederick Morton, published by Secker and

Warburg Ltd; to Miss Elsie M. Rose, for permission to quote from *Fifty Years Ago* and *Good Neighbours*, by Walter Rose; to Mrs Elsie S. Mitchell, for permission to quote from *Two Lectures on the History of Whitchurch*, by Joseph Holloway; to Joyce Donald, for permission to reprint extracts from *A Short History of Long Crendon*; to R. W. Wainwright, Esq., L.C.P., Headmaster of Ludgershall C. of E. Primary School, for permission to quote from the *Ludgershall Gazette*; to Cambridge University Press, for permission to reprint the poem, 'My County', by H. Evelyn Howard (originally published by permission of Mrs Ralph Howard) from *Landmarks* edited by G. R. Hamilton and John Arlott; to William Collins, Sons and Company, Ltd, for permission to reprint the extract from *The Lion and the Unicorn*, by Sir Arthur Bryant, C.H., C.B.E.; to Laurence Pollinger Ltd, for permission to use extracts from 'Hedge Chequerwork' from *The Face of England*, by H. E. Bates, published by B. T. Batsford Ltd; to Sir Isaac Pitman and Sons, Ltd, for permission to reprint the poem 'King Charles the First' by Hugh Chesterman, from *Speech Practice*, edited by G. Colson; to Souvenir Press Ltd, for permission to quote from *The Gazetteer of British Ghosts*, by Peter Underwood; to Geoffrey Grigson, for permission to reprint the extract from his *Herbal of All Sorts*, published by Phoenix House; to David Higham Associates, Ltd, for permission to reprint the poem 'Quainton Churchyard' from *The World's Room*, by Laurence Whistler, published by William Heinemann Ltd.

The photographs on pages 17, 40, 45, 53, 57, 63, 96, 107, and 127 are by Ronald Goodearl; on pages 21, 29 and 35 by Peter Newbolt; on pages 47, 67 and 109 by Frank H. Meads; on pages 27, 70 and 104 by J. Parminter, Aylesbury Camera Club; on page 51 by Mary Ellen Haig; on page 75 by C. W. F. Holmes; on page 111 by J. R. Fairman; on page 115 by Sybil Clarke, Aylesbury Camera Club. The photograph on page 33 is reproduced by courtesy of the County Museum, Aylesbury; the photograph of Wotton House on page 79 by courtesy of Mrs Patrick Brunner; of Waddesdon Manor on page 99 by courtesy of the National Trust, Waddesdon; and of Dorton House on page 132 by courtesy of Ashfold School. The drawings on pages 44, 87 and 113 are by Edward Stamp; the drawing of Dunton Church on page 134 was made by John Piper for the Wing Airport Resistance Association, and is reproduced by permission of Desmond Fennell, Q.C.

Index

Figures in italics indicate illustrations

Ascott, 136
Ashendon, 84, 136
Askett, 136
Aston Abbotts, 89, 136
Aston Clinton, 69, 84, 137
Aston Sandford, 137
Aubrey Fletcher Family, 139
Aubrey Fletcher, Sir Henry, 141
Aubrey, Sir John, 19, 132
Aylesbury, 13–14, 18, 26–28, 35, 40–48, 52, 62, 65–66, 73, 78, 85, 88, 90, 92, 103, 120, 137

Bates, H. E., 64
Bell, Michael Farrar, 137
Beresford, Jane, 48, 114–115
Berkshire, Buckinghamshire and Oxfordshire Naturalists Trust, 80–81
Bernwood, Forest of, 19, 20, 108, 136, 138, 145, 151
Betjeman, Sir John, 121, 137
Bierton, 88, 138
Biggs, John, 42, 140
Bishopstone, 48, 122–123, 125, 138
Bledlow, 138
Boarstall, 19, 80, 138
Boarstall Cartulary, 19
Boarstall Duck Decoy, 81, 138
Bolebec Castle, 150
Bolebec, Walter Gifford de, 23
Boleyn, Anne, 26, 28–29
Boleyn, Thomas, 28
Bourdillon, Thomas, 72
Brewer, J. Norris, 14
Brill, 18, 20, 34, 52, 111–112, 128, 138–139

Brill & Wotton Tramway, 111–112
Brooke, Rupert, 121
Bryant, Sir Arthur, 6–8, 108, 135, 136, 139
Buchanan, Sir Colin, 133
Buckingham, 40, 46, 91, 136
Buckingham, Duke of, 85
Buckland, 139

Catherine of Aragon, 28, 92–93
Charles I, 34–38, 39, 41, 141, 142, 144, 149
Charles II, 41, 85
Chearsley, 48, 80, 139
Cheddington, 80, 139
Chequers, 129–130, 137, 141, 142, 148
Chesterman, Hugh, 39
Chilterns, The, 15–18, 35, 80, 128, 131, 133, 136, 138, 141, 150
Chilterns, The, 121
Chilton, 89, 136, 139
Churchill, Sir Winston, 100
Claydon House, *104*
Claydons, The, 80, 92, 104–105, 117, 139
Colet, Dr John, 25
Cowdy, Susan, 62, 81, 90
Creslow, 51, 85–86, 139
Cromwell, Oliver, 28, 34, 41, 147
Cromwell, Thomas, 25
Cublington, 51, 89, 120, 131, 140
Cublington Spinney, 140
Cuddington, 28, 48–50, 89, 106, 140

Davies, Max, 62
Defoe, Daniel, 47

157

Dinton, 41–42, 48, 50, 89, 140
Disraeli, Benjamin, 93–94
Doddershall, 80, 141
Donald, Joyce, 43, 113
Dorton, 128, 141
Dorton House, *132*
Drayton Beauchamp, 141
Drayton, Michael, 33
Dunton, 89, 120, 134, 141

Edgcott, 141
Edward the Confessor, 18–19, 20, 138
Eland, G., 32, 85
Elizabeth I, 29, 85, 89, 92, 148, 151
Elizabeth II, 138, 149
Ellesborough, 89, 102, 141
Eythrope, 116–117, 126, 142

Fawcett, William, 78
Fennel, Desmond, 134
Fitter, Richard, 81
Fleet Marston, 89, 142
Ford, 48, 80, 142
Fowler, J. F. K., 29, 68, 75, 94, 111

Gerard, Geoffrey, 26
Gibbs, Robert, 19, 34, 40, 44, 56, 112
Gibraltar, 142
Gladstone, William Ewart, 85
Gomme, G. L., 70
Good, Norman, 50
Grandborough, 46, 142
Great Hampden, 34–36
Great Horwood, 33, 54–55
Great Kimble, 34, 89, 142
Grendon Underwood, 80, 142

Haddenham, 42, 48–50, 55, 70–71, 80, 143
Hampden, John, 34–35, 37, 39, 40, 44, 89, 142, 149
Hardwick, 89, 130, 143

Harman, H., 128
Hartwell, 73–74, 117, 122, 143
Hartwell House, *75*
Hartwell, Lower, 144
Henry I, 23
Henry II, 20
Henry VI, 19, 26
Henry VIII, 24, 26, 28, 85, 92, 140
Hoggeston, 34, 120, 144
Hogshaw, 144
Holloway, Joseph, 23, 51, 57
Holyman, John, 28, 140
Horsenden, 144
Howard, H. Evelyn, 129
Howie, Anne Craig, 69, 93
Hulcott, 89, 144

Ickford, 34, 144
Ilmer, 144
Ivinghoe Beacon, 16, 131

James, Anne, 36

Keach, Benjamin, 45–46
Kingsey, 145
Kingswood, 20, 145

Lee, Family, 88, 89, 137, 144, 148
Lee, Lord and Lady, of Fareham, 129–130
Lee, Lady Margaret, 130
Leland, 136
Lipscomb, Dr George, 56, 57, 136, 145, 148
Long Crendon, 42, 43, 48, 50, 57–62, 69, 70, 80, 113, 145
Long Marston, 145
Lonsdale, Earl of, 108–111
Louis XVIII, 73–75, 143
Ludgershall, 19–23, 47, 145

MacDonell, A. G., 14
Mansfield, Estrith, 23
Marsh, 123, 124, 145

Marsh Gibbon, 146
Martyn, John, 47
Massingham, H. J., 102
Mayne, Simon, 41–42, 140
Meadle, 146
Melbourne, Lord, 102
Mentmore, 146
Monks Risborough, 146
Morton, Frederick, 100

Napoleon Bonaparte, 73, 74
Nield, John Camden, 68–69, 146
Nigel the Huntsman, 19, 138
Nightingale, Florence, 102–106
North Marston, 23–25, 52, 68–69, 146
Notley Abbey, 23, 69, 139

Oakley, 147
Osyth, St, 18
Oving, 62, 131–132, 147
Owlswick, 147

Piddington, 147
Pitchcott, 132, 147
Princes Risborough, 84, 147

Quainton, 14, 52–54, 55–56, 72, 89, 131, 148
Quainton Churchyard, 130
Quarrendon, 18, 89, 129, 148

Rayner, Eric, 42
Reynolds, Ruth, 55, 122
Rodger, Ian, 18
Rose, Walter, 72, 98
Roskill Commission, 44, 131, 135
Rothschild, Baron Ferdinand de, 98–100, 108, 111, 147
Rouse, E. Clive, 90
Rowsham, 148
Royal Bucks Hospital, 103
Rupert, Prince, 34–35, 43–44

Scott, Thomas, 137
Sedrup, 148
Shabbington, 80, 148
Shorne, John, 23–25, 146
Soulbury, 119, 121, 148
Spencer-Bernard Family, 115, 146
Stewkley, 54, 88, 120, 148
Stoke Hammond, 148
Stoke Mandeville, 34, 36, 122, 149
Stone, 124, 149
Swanbourne, 40, 121, 149

Taylor, Frederick J., 119
Terrick House, 149
Thame, 43, 46–47, 113, 149
Thame, River, 47, 60, 80, 117
Tring (Reservoir), 81

Underwood, Peter, 87
Upton, 150
Uttley, Alison, 28

Verney Family, 139
Verney, Parthenope, 8, 102–103
Verney, Margaret, 18, 25, 46
Verney, Ralph B., 44
Verney, Sir Harry, 106
Verney, Sir Ralph, 36–38
Victoria, Queen, 68–69, 100, 146
Vince, John N. T., 55
Viney, Col. Oscar, 138

Waddesdon, 66, 80, 84, 89, 132, 150
Waddesdon Manor, 98–100, *99*
Weedon, 150
Westcar, John, 51, 140, 151
Westlington, 150
Weston Turville, 150
Wharton, Lord Philip, 33
Whistler, Laurence, 131
Whistler, Rex, 131, 151
Whitchurch, 23, 51, 53, 56–57, 90, 120, 132, 150
Whiteleaf Cross, 151

William the Conqueror, 14, 19, 20, 23, 138, 145, 150
Wilmot, Chester, 65
Winchendon, 33, 47, 89
Winchendon, Upper, 84
Winchendon, Nether, 48, 50
Winchendon, Nether, House, *115*

Wing, 16, 88, 120, 151
Wingrave, 151
Winslow, 45–46, 121
Wotton House, 79, 151
Wotton Lakes, 81, 118
Wotton Underwood, 151
Wycliffe, John, 19–23, 145

Buckinghamshire, reproduced from Christopher Saxton's map, engraved by William Hole for Camden's Britannia, 1610

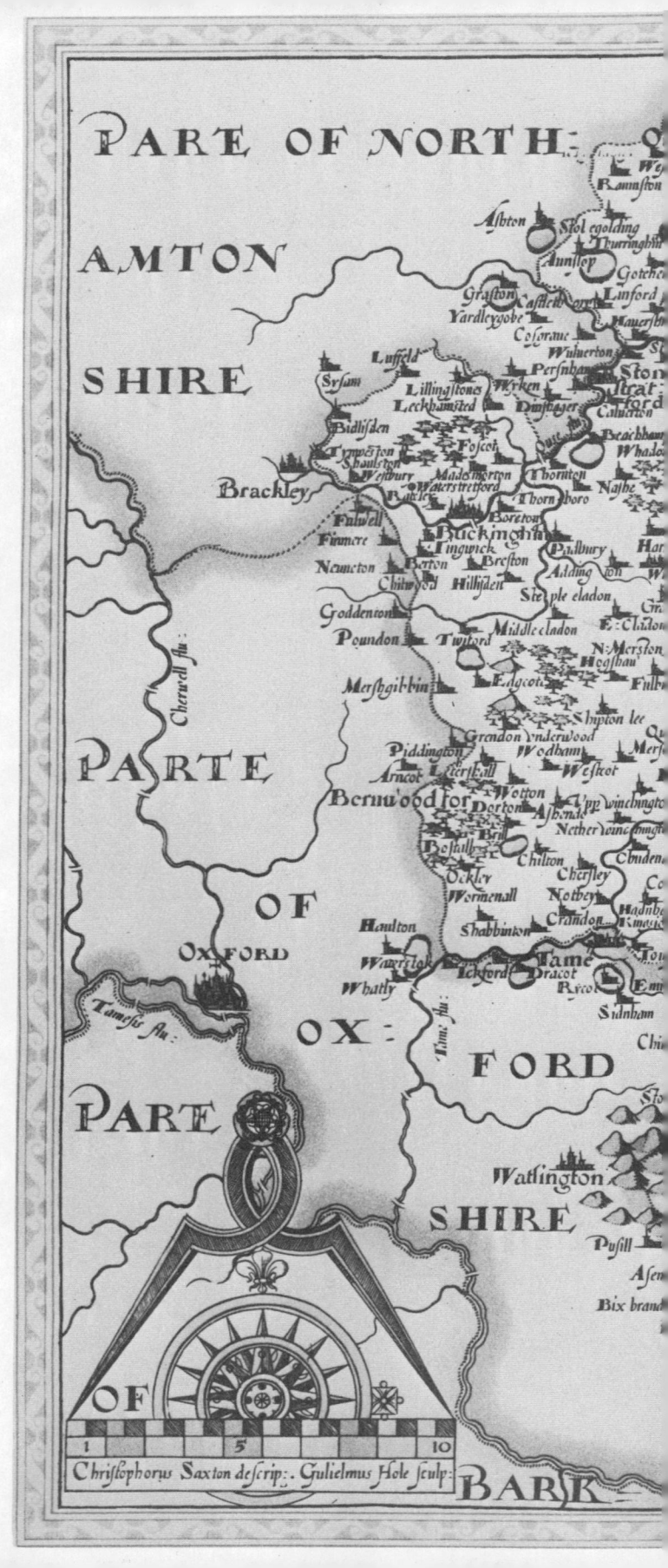